American Statesmen

EDITED BY

JOHN T. MORSE, JR.

American Statesmen

ALEXANDER HAMILTON

BY

HENRY CABOT LODGE

GREENWOOD PRESS, PUBLISHERS
NEW YORK

Originally published in 1917
by the Houghton Mifflin Company

First Greenwood Reprinting 1969

Library of Congress Catalogue Card Number 69-13974

SBN 8371-1928-6

PRINTED IN UNITED STATES OF AMERICA

EDITOR'S PREFACE

In the history of the United States, Washington and Lincoln stand apart in a monumental solitude. They belong in no class; no one seeks a place near them, or challenges even a possible comparison with them. It is only after we have established them in this grand and undisputed isolation that we try to put our other statesmen into ranks and classes according to our judgment of their capacity and their services. This attitude of these two men is a peculiarity in our annals distinguishing us from other peoples. No other nation has heroes filling quite the like relationship. The nearest approach to it is furnished by William of Orange. Neither Julius Cæsar nor Napoleon Bonaparte are parallel instances, though they overshadowed respectively all other Romans and Frenchmen; they were greater than others, yet they could be compared and measured with others. But this cannot be done with either Washington or Lincoln, because, apart from greatness, they are *different* from others.

When we come to make out the list of our
statesmen of the first rank, Alexander Hamilton would probably receive at least a plurality
of votes for the highest place. In the minds of
his countrymen, his memory has always been
surrounded with a brilliant halo, has always had
a prestige which may be regarded as in some
respects surprising. For when readers come
down to the actual records of his career, they
find that they have to hear chiefly of financial
schemes, the management of the treasury, arrangements concerning the national debt, reve-
nues, tariffs, and internal taxation — dry matters, for the most part, and not often enticing
popular interest. None the less it is the case
that our historical writers have found a singular
fascination about Hamilton ; the amount of literature and the consequent research concerning
him have been very great : yet there is not any
symptom of satiety ; our people still eagerly
seize upon everything which is written as to his
career, and seem unable to hear enough of the
subject. Such a condition cannot be accounted
for by the tradition of his personal beauty of
countenance and charm of manner, which made
him a leader of the leaders in public life, neither
by the interesting tale of his tragic death. The
explanation and the truth lie far deeper. Ham-

ilton's fame indicates the unformulated but full appreciation of the unquestionable historic fact that he was the real maker of the government of the United States. Washington created, or at least caused to be created, the national entity; Hamilton did actually create the political[1] entity.

By reason of these facts, the life of Hamilton was sure to be one of the most important volumes of this series; and, since so much careful writing had been already done concerning him, the selection of his biographer demanded more than ordinary consideration. No one in the country had at that time made a more thorough study of Federalism than Mr. Lodge had done. His ancestor, George Cabot, had been one of the chiefs of the Federalist party in its stronghold of New England, and had been the intimate friend of Hamilton; and the testimony of the intimacy still lives upon Mr. Lodge's library wall in the shape of Trumbull's portrait of Hamilton, a present to George Cabot as a near and dear friend. Knowing well that, if Mr. Lodge was very naturally inclined to make a hero of Hamilton, he at least practiced a strictly intelligent and reasonable worship, I

---

[1] I regret to be obliged to use this now degraded word, but I use it in its original and proper classic signification.

was greatly pleased to have him accept the task
of writing the volume, which has fulfilled my
expectations in every respect. It is a just as
well as a sympathetic biography. Since writing it, Mr. Lodge has edited the new edition of
Hamilton's works; and it is not supposable that
any writer will hereafter have access to any important materials which he has not had and
used.

                                    JOHN T. MORSE, JR.
September, 1898.

CONTENTS

CHAP.   PAGE

    I. Boyhood and Youth 1

   II. The Revolution 13

  III. Law and Politics 31

  IV. The Constitution 49

   V. The Treasury and the Financial Policy . 83

  VI. The Results of the Financial Policy . 115

  VII. Party Contests 134

VIII. Foreign Relations and the Maintenance of
         the Authority of the Government . . 151

  IX. The Jay Treaty and the Adams Adminis-
         tration 185

   X. Professional Life. — Duel and Death . 234

Appendix 283

Index 297

ALEXANDER HAMILTON

CHAPTER I

BOYHOOD AND YOUTH

ON the eleventh day of January in the year 1757, the wife of a Scotch merchant in the island of Nevis gave birth to a son, who received the name of Alexander Hamilton.[1] Many varying elements were mingled in this boy. He was a British subject born in the tropics, Scotch on his father's side and of French Huguenot descent on his mother's, and to this conjunction many of the qualities which Hamilton exhibited in after life may be traced. But that which strikes us most at the outset is his extraordinary precocity; his mind and character seemed to partake of the nature of those luxuriant tropical plants which in a few months attain a growth permitted only after years of conflict and care in the harsher climate of the North. Upon the childhood of Hamilton even the exhaustive and

[1] See Appendix, Note A.

devoted labors of his son and biographer, Mr. John C. Hamilton, fail to throw much light. His mother, who apparently possessed an unusual degree of wit and beauty, died early. His father was unsuccessful in business, and Alexander, the only surviving child, fell to the care of maternal relations, among whom he picked up a rude, odd, and desultory sort of education, and by whom he was placed in a counting-room before he was twelve years old.

There at his clerkly desk we catch the first clear glimpse of the future statesman in the well-known letter addressed to his friend Edward Stevens : " I contemn the groveling condition of a clerk, or the like," he says, " to which my fortune condemns me, and would willingly risk my life, though not my character, to exalt my station. I am confident, Ned, that my youth excludes me from any hopes of immediate preferment, nor do I desire it ; but I mean to prepare the way for futurity." The expression savors of the grandiloquence of the last century, but the thought is natural and even sober, and is, moreover, that of a man, and yet it was uttered by a boy who had not passed his thirteenth birthday. At the same tender age he was left in charge of his employer's affairs, and some of his correspondence of that time has been preserved to us. These clear and sensible letters of business have nothing in themselves unusual, but it is not a little remarkable that they should be the work of a lad whose contemporaries were studying the rudiments of grammar on school benches, while his capacity was great enough not only to write such letters but practically to manage on his own responsibility the affairs of a considerable merchant.

In the intervals of his office work Hamilton read and wrote much; Pope and Plutarch, we are told, were his favorite authors, and to his exercises in composition was due the publication of a vivid account of a severe hurricane which raged with devastating force in the West Indies. This literary effort attracted a good deal of attention, especially among those vague relatives to whom the boy's interests were intrusted, and by them it was decided that so much talent deserved wider opportunities than could be found in a West Indian counting-house. Funds were provided, and in his fifteenth year Hamilton bade a final adieu to his birthplace and took ship for Boston, where he arrived in October, 1772. Thence he proceeded to New York, and there, thanks to letters from the excellent Dr. Knox, a Presbyterian clergyman of Nevis, and one of the boy's earliest friends, he found wise and good counselors. By their advice he entered a grammar school of some note at Eliza-

bethtown, where he extended his acquaintance,
and during the winter pursued his studies with
the fiery and unresting energy so characteristic
of him throughout his life. At odd moments
he indulged in his propensity for writing. He
produced not only prose but poetry, including
hymns, elegies, and verses of all sorts, which
were not without the merit inseparable from the
work of an active, fresh, and fertile mind. At
the end of the year he was ready for college.
His first thought was for Princeton, but, as he
characteristically proposed to go through the
course as rapidly as he could without regard
to classes, the rules of the college would not
permit his admittance, and he entered King's
College in New York, where he prosecuted his
studies with the aid of a private tutor as fast
as he wished. In the university as at school
he threw himself heart and soul into his work,
gathering up knowledge with quick apprehension, while the tireless activity of his mind continually sent his thoughts ranging into other and
wider fields of finance, government, and politics.
It was then his custom of an afternoon, as we
are told, to walk under the shadow of the trees
on Batteau Street, plunged in thought and talking eagerly to himself. The passers-by would
turn to look at the small, slight youth, still a
mere boy in appearance, dark of skin and with

deep-set eyes ; and those who knew the " young West Indian," as he was called, already specu- lated about him vaguely, as people are wont to do about those who give or seem to give obvious promise of an illustrious future. But while Hamilton was leading the reflective life of a student, and meditating beneath the shadow of the trees, imbued perhaps with the " prophetic soul of the wide world, dreaming of things to come," a great revolution was swiftly coming to its crisis about him.

Successful men are those who take advantage of their opportunities, for opportunities are not made by men, but for them. Hamilton, we may be sure, would have taken full advantage of any and every opportunity, but he had the good for- tune to have a great one opened to him. The question was which side in the gathering con- flict he would espouse. It seemed perhaps more difficult to Hamilton to decide then than it does to us to decide for him now; and yet his choice was simple and his selection inevitable. He was singularly free in making his decision. He was born, it is true, in a little English dependency and had always been a provincial, but he had no family in New York to warp or incumber him; his ties of friendship were new and probably as much with one side as the other; and he was to all intents and purposes his own master. A

visit in the spring of 1774 to Boston, the hotbed
of resistance to England and possessing an at-
mosphere very different from that of New York,
where the Tories were in the ascendant, probably affected him not a little, and led him to a
close examination of the all-absorbing controversy. He himself tells us that he had formed
" strong prejudices on the ministerial side until
he became convinced by the superior force of
the arguments in favor of the colonial claims."
This explanation is exceedingly characteristic
and highly instructive. His masterful temper
and innate love and respect for government,
order, and strong rule dictated his prejudices.
His clear, vigorous mind, and his profound belief in reasoning and argument, which so prevailed with him always, showed him plainly that
the colonies were in the right. But after every
allowance for the conviction brought by reason,
an instinctive sense of what must be the true
path for him to follow undoubtedly played a
large part in Hamilton's decision. He was
young, unknown, an adventurer in a strange
land, and burning with a lofty ambition. The
world was before him, and his fortune, which he
meant should be a great one, was to be made.
Constituted authority and a continuity of government offered at best but little to the most
successful provincial. Change, revolution, and

war might bring almost anything in the way of military or civic glory. He chose rightly, and he also chose wisely, when he cast in his lot with the opponents of England.

New York was in possession of the Tories. The Assembly was ministerial, narrow-minded, and with a majority controlled by the home government. Upon this Assembly, in order to force New York into line with the other colonies now preparing for the first Congress, it was decided to bring what in these days would be called "pressure." With this purpose a great meeting in the fields was held on July 6, 1774, under the auspices of the patriot leaders. Hamilton was present listening to the orators. Like the boy Pitt under the gallery of the House of Commons, Hamilton was impressed by what was left unsaid far more than by all the rhetoric of the speakers. Filled with the belief that he could supply the omissions which he detected, he made his way to the platform and stood before the people. There were a few moments of youthful embarrassment and hesitation, while the crowd stared at the audacious boy, and then nature asserted itself and his words flowed unchecked. Hamilton was never eloquent in the sense in which Chatham or Mirabeau or Henry were eloquent, for he had not the imaginative and poetical temperament. But he had the elo-

quence of sound reason and clear logic, combined
with great power and lucidity of expression, and
backed by a strong and passionate nature.   As
he poured out with all his young fervor thoughts
long pent up in his breast, we can well believe
that the crowd, murmuring " It is a collegian !
it is a collegian ! " were deeply stirred by the
oratory of one who spoke so well, although he
was a stranger and in appearance a mere boy.

Once embarked, Hamilton was too honorable,
too high-minded, and too thoroughly satisfied of
the soundness of his convictions ever to waver
or turn back, and tempting offers from the other
side at a later day, when his value and his
powers were better known, passed idly by him.
He was not only firm of purpose, but, having
taken his part, he pushed on in every direction
open to him with his accustomed zeal.   In those
days public opinion was formed and the power
of the press exerted through pamphlets, or by
essays addressed to the printer, and published
by him in his newspaper as communications.
The ablest men of the country employed these
channels to reach the public mind, and great
importance was attached to such productions.
Two tracts of considerable force assailing Congress and its measures, and written by two of
the ablest writers on the Tory side, appeared in
the autumn of 1774.   The effect of these pam-

phlets was severe to the patriots, and while they
were casting about for a champion Hamilton
answered the attack. The Tories replied, and
Hamilton rejoined in a second pamphlet of some
seventy-eight pages. Both these tracts, which
showed marked ability, were variously attributed
to the most eminent leaders, and when their
authorship was known the young writer gained
a wide and immediate reputation. To argue
points of constitutional law and of political justice and expediency was above all things con-
genial to Hamilton with his already well-stored
mind, acute logic, and capacity for discussion.
The pamphlets were excellent of their kind at
a time when such performances were strictly
judged, and, taken in connection with the youth
of the author, deserved the great success which
they obtained. They gave Hamilton an assured
position, and led to the rejected offers from the
Tories to which allusion has just been made.

The winter of 1775 passed away, New York
was at last forced into the Congress, the battles
came in Massachusetts, and revolution began.
Meanwhile Hamilton continued his arguments
against England in vigorous newspaper essays,
took part in public meetings, and devoted his
time to a study of military affairs, seeking also
for practical experience by joining a volunteer
corps commanded by Major Fleming. Besides

showing nerve in the performance of some trying military duties which were becoming very
necessary in those troublous times, Hamilton
appeared prominently on several occasions in
efforts to repress, by argument and by fearless
personal exposure, outbreaks of mob violence.
The most memorable of these occasions was one
which happened during the disturbances caused
by the British ship of war Asia opening fire
on the town. Persons and property had been
injured, and there was wild commotion and an
angry rising of the people in New York. The
king's storehouse was pillaged, the Connecticut
troops were sent for, and Liberty Boys rushed
through the streets, threatening outrage and
ruin to every Tory. Most prominent among
the adherents of the Crown was Dr. Cooper,
president of the college, and thither the angry
mob hurried, bent on mischief of a desperate
sort. When they arrived they found Hamilton
and his friend Troup on the steps of the building ready to delay their entrance. The former
at once stepped forward and began to reason
vigorously with the crowd, and to denounce
their disorderly conduct. While Hamilton was
thus engaged, and while the populace halted to
listen with amazement, no doubt, to the eager
words of a youth whom they had last seen exposed to the fire of the Asia occupied with other

patriots in removing cannon, the excellent Dr.
Cooper fled, after warning the people from a
high window not to be guided by such a mad-
man as his former pupil who was then address-
ing them.

The doctor's mistake was natural enough.
He could not believe that Hamilton, patriot and
rebel, was resisting the people and restraining
their violence for the sake of an old Tory clergyman. There is, indeed, something rather surprising as well as quite fine in the spectacle thus
presented of a boy, whose blood was hot with
the new strong wine of revolution, risking his
life and, what he loved probably much more, his
influence and his popularity, in behalf of law,
order, and mercy. In a similar fashion he interfered to save the life of one Thurman from what
was then known as "Travis's mob;" and when
the Connecticut horse broke into the town and
carried off the types of Rivington, the Tory
printer, Hamilton was filled with indignation at
this violent suppression of opinion, and, if he
could have got a few men to go with him, would
have ridden after the marauders and recaptured
the property. These instances of self-restraint
and cool bravery are all remarkable in so young
and so enthusiastic a man as Hamilton. In the
midst of revolutionary excitement he did not
hesitate to come forward to check his own party,

to oppose and censure their excesses, to take the side of the unpopular minority in behalf of mercy, justice, order, free speech, and a free press. But whether he succeeded or failed in these attempts they were creditable alike to his sense and courage; they show strongly his early and deep detestation of anything like disorder, and above all his hatred of that most noxious of all forms of confusion, a riotous city rabble.

But the time for preparation was closing fast. Early in 1776 the New York convention ordered a company of artillery to be raised. Hamilton applied for the command, and his examination quickly dispelled the doubts of his fitness in those who suspected mere youthful presumption. He recruited his company rapidly, and spent upon its equipment his second and last remittance from home. He had now burned his ships behind him. Youth, study, and the days of dreaming and meditation were gone. He was a man striving for everything that an ambitious man can desire. He had already entered upon the stage of life at an age when most boys were still in school or college, and a very exciting and bustling drama he found in progress. He had youth, health, great talent, a strong will, courage, ambition, and his sword. With these weapons his fortune was to be made.

CHAPTER II

THE REVOLUTION

THE artillery company quickly showed the talent of its commander. Hamilton devoted himself to it as he did to everything he undertook, and by unceasing drill soon made its evolutions conspicuous in an army where discipline was novel and models were rare. The young captain, by the excellence of his troop, attracted the attention of Greene, who fell into conversation with him, was impressed by his ability, and introduced him to Washington, thus putting him at this early day in the line of advancement. The kindness of the Rhode Island general was never forgotten by Hamilton, who became one of Greene's strongest supporters and warmest admirers, at a later day declaring him to have been the first soldier of the Revolution. Hamilton, however, was soon tested by a severer experience than any which drill or parade could offer. He won his spurs at the disastrous battle of Long Island, where with great coolness and courage he brought up the rear in the masterly retreat which saved the army, and gave the first

conspicuous proof of that daring and sagacious
genius for which Washington was as eminent in
good as in evil fortune. With the rest of the
army Hamilton took part in the retreat up the
Hudson, distinguished himself by the admirable
manner in which he served his battery at White
Plains, and offered to recover by storm Fort
Washington, — a piece of reckless daring to
which Washington refused his consent. From
New York Hamilton went with the army in their
terrible march through New Jersey, and shared
in the brilliant campaign of Trenton and Princeton. By this time, after six months of hard
fighting, his company was reduced to twenty-
five men, who retained their old discipline, but
little else. Their commander had, however,
made a name as a dashing and gallant officer,
and this, added to his literary reputation, led to
his appointment as one of Washington's aides
with the rank of lieutenant-colonel, on March 1,
1777, when he was barely twenty years old.

Hamilton acted wisely in accepting this new
position, for which he was peculiarly fitted. He
seems to have regarded the step with some misgiving, and to have felt that he had made a
considerable sacrifice. His self-confidence, natural enough under the circumstances, was then
as always too strong; but in this instance he
controlled it. Extraordinary success and the

consciousness of great talents made it easy for a
very young man to believe that if he remained
in the line nothing was beyond his reach, and
that no prospect was too brilliant for reasonable
hope. Yet it is more than probable that if he
had continued a line officer he would have attained no higher rank than that which he ultimately reached, while he would have sacrificed
experiences and connections of inestimable value.
With all his precocity and undoubted aptitude
for military affairs, he was still too young to
have obtained the highest commands before the
end of the war, whereas, as a member of Washington's family, he was brought into close asso-
ciation with the greatest man of the age, whose
friendship he was able to win and retain. As a
member of the staff of the commander-in-chief,
Hamilton's duties were various and highly responsible. He did not have the independent
command for which he sighed, but he was present
at all the battles in which the army was engaged,
took more or less part in them, and always
gained honor and distinction. His principal
occupation was in the conduct of Washington's
immense correspondence. A large proportion
of the endless letters, reports, and proclamations
which issued from headquarters was the work of
Hamilton. In regard to these documents there
has been a very needless discussion. To claim

for Hamilton the merit of all the correspondence which bears Washington's name, but which
is in the handwriting of his aide-de-camp, and
to speak of it as if Hamilton was the man who
directed the movements of armies and informed
Congress of their duty, is absurd. Washington
was fortunate in having on his staff one of the
most brilliant men of the day, with a vigorous,
original, and well-stored mind, fertile in thought,
a lucid and acute reasoner, and a master of a
clear and forcible style. We may be sure that
nothing passed through Hamilton's hands without being put in the strongest and most condensed form, and at the same time amplified and
adorned; but we may be equally sure that, however much the general profited by the suggestions of his able secretary, the central ideas and
guiding principles, whether conveyed in a word
or dictated at length, were the intellectual property of the man who signed those letters and
reports with the name of George Washington.
The kernel of a letter may lie in a simple nega-
tive or affirmative, which when fully expressed
will cover pages, but the author of the letter is
he who directs the decisive "yes" or "no," and
not the man who clothes the thought in fitting
words. This in no sense implies detraction. It
is a wrong to any man, be he great or small, to
attribute to him something to which he is not

entitled, and to present Hamilton, even in the most indirect way, as the author of Washington's dispatches, is merely to injure the former and neither to hurt nor help the latter. Hamilton's work as military secretary — and there is a great mass of it extant — deserves all praise, and greatly redounds to his credit. As his enthusiastic comrade, the gallant Laurens, said, he certainly held the pen of Junius in the American army, and to that gifted pen, employed as freely in another's service as in his own, and to the versatile and original mind of its possessor, Washington owed much and gave every proof that he appreciated the debt. For those interested in a close study of Hamilton's mind and character, the dispatches which he wrote as secretary, as well as those which he composed in his individual capacity, are of great value. In them we can trace the rapid development of a keen and powerful intellect. There we can see displayed sagacity, foresight, acuteness, and force in every affair to which they relate, whether military or civil. There, too, we perceive the fertility of resource, the vigorous self-confidence, unhesitating decision and undaunted spirit, which the young aide afterwards made conspicuous on broader fields. All these qualities — and they form a goodly list — were moreover in a state of vigorous growth. There is nothing in Hamil-

ton to suggest his namesake who bore the famous
sobriquet of "single speech," who was content
with one splendid effort and then silent forever.
Hamilton's correspondence, on the contrary,
during his service on Washington's staff, constantly improves. In this and in many other
ways he shows that reserved force which is one
of the most essential elements of greatness, and
the capacity to gather increased strength, like
Antæus, from each fresh contact with the earth
of every-day events in a time of strain and trial.

The most important duty which fell to Hamilton while serving as an aide was his mission to
Gates to seek reinforcements. At that moment
additional troops were essential to Washington,
and they were only to be obtained from the
northern army. While Washington was bearing
defeat, and fighting on with grim pertinacity,
Gates, in command of an army formed from
the hardy levies of the North, had achieved a
signal victory which has taken a place among
the fifteen decisive battles of the world's history. The surrender of Burgoyne had made
Gates — to whom as little was due for the victory as could well be the case with the commanding officer — the idol of the North, and
of New England especially. To offend Gates
personally was a small matter, but to offend
the northern colonies, just then dissatisfied with

Washington, would have been a very serious affair. As the superior officer of Gates, Washington had the right to command, and at the same time this was precisely what he wished to avoid. Hamilton was, therefore, to get the troops without using, except in the last resort, the imperative authority which he carried in his pocket. It was a delicate and difficult mission. Hamilton was never conspicuous for the patient and tolerant qualities which make a great diplomat, least of all in the days of impetuous youth, and yet, thanks to his strong sense and clear perception of facts, he acquitted himself most admirably. Gates, naturally a weak man, was blinded by the glamour of his great victory. When the wishes of the commander-in-chief were made known to him he held back, hesitated, and finally gave way. Hamilton got his troops by the exercise of much patient persistence, and kept the tempting letter of command out of sight. On his way back he also pushed forward the delaying Putnam, treating that general much more cavalierly than Gates, but only, it is to be feared, as the unmanageable temper of the old wolf-killer deserved. Hamilton won much credit, as well as the approbation of Washington, for his excellent behavior on this occasion. Not long afterward he was sent to Newport on a similar

mission to the French, and again he showed himself a good envoy, although he failed to bring
our allies to accede to Washington's wishes.

One other episode of Hamilton's career as an
aide-de-camp deserves notice in any account of
his life. His position brought him into close
connection with the wretched attempt to betray
West Point. It fell to him to see and strive
to console Mrs. Arnold in the first agony of her
distress after the flight of her traitor husband,
and it was his lot also to be much with the
gifted and ill-fated André. In letters to Miss
Schuyler, his future wife, he depicted the scene
with Mrs. Arnold; he described the whole unhappy affair, and dwelt much upon André and
upon his expiation of another's crime in which
he had been but a tool. In all this there was
deep pathos, and it acquires a fresh interest for
the student of Hamilton's character as it shows
the deep feeling and tenderness of his nature.
No account of Arnold's treason and of the ac-
tors in it has ever equaled Hamilton's letters,
which in their clear and forcible sentences are
full of a subdued eloquence, touching us and
appealing to us even now by the emotion of a
strong and reserved nature.

Such, in brief, were the salient events in
Hamilton's experience of four years as a member of Washington's staff. But not the least

striking incident of this period of his life was
that which resulted in the sudden close of his
service with the commander-in-chief. We have
Hamilton's own account of the affair, written
on February 18, 1781, two days after it happened. Washington had sent for Hamilton to
come to him. The latter, delaying a few minutes in obeying, found the general at the head
of the stairs, who reproved him with no undue
sharpness, saying that to keep him waiting was
a mark of disrespect. Whereupon Hamilton
replied, " I am not conscious of it, sir ; but since
you have thought it, we part." One can hardly
read this youthful ebullition even now without
a smile. The fashion has prevailed of treating
this quarrel as if the two participants stood upon
equal ground, and this puts the whole matter
on a thoroughly false footing. Let us look at
the pair a moment as they stand there at the
head of the stairs in the New Windsor house.
One is a boy in years, although of unusual and
manly maturity of mind. He is a stranger
in the land who has shown himself possessed
of great and promising talents ; he has proved
himself an able writer, a brave soldier, an excellent secretary. This small, slight, dark-eyed
stripling is facing George Washington, and
brimming over with a sense of offended dignity.
Washington stands there in the prime of his

middle age, large and imposing in personal appearance. He is one of the foremost men in the world, a great general and statesman, grave and impressive as becomes a man who has carried in his hands the life of a nation. Some of Hamilton's biographers have referred to this affair as one of Washington's outbursts of passion. Like all great men Washington had strong passions, like very few great men he had them under almost complete control. When they did break forth, as happened now and then in great stress of feeling, they bent everything before them, and there was a hush among those who listened. If Washington had spoken to Hamilton as he did to Lear about St. Clair's defeat, that fine reply, one is inclined to think, would not have been uttered. But deep waters are ruffled, not stirred, by a passing breeze. Washington spoke to Hamilton in a tone of sharp but proper reproof. Few generals, probably, would have spoken so courteously and gently to a young aide, who had kept them waiting, and thus sinned against the first of military virtues, prompt obedience. The event in itself is trivial enough. We smile at Hamilton's dignity, and at his youthful satisfaction with his own conduct; but Washington's behavior, then and subsequently, is not without importance. He not only endeavored at once to heal the breach, although Hamilton repelled his advances, but he continued to interest himself in his former aide, and suffered their friendship to undergo no diminution. There was more in this than the magnanimity, absolutely without flaw, which Washington always showed. It was a tribute to Hamilton's abilities from one of the best judges of men who ever lived. He saw Hamilton's capacity; he cared nothing for his little outburst; and he was determined to retain his hold upon one in whom he perceived the possibility of great service to the country at some future time. He did this, too, without advancing Hamilton over the heads of other men to the position which the latter felt he would have gained if he had not joined the staff.[1] Washington watched over his fortunes at Yorktown, where Hamilton had a command and obtained the perilous privilege of leading the assault upon one of the outworks of the enemy. The opportunity was not lost. At the head of his men Hamilton rushed with all his fiery impetuosity upon the British redoubt, carried all before him and took the position in ten minutes, doing his work much more quickly than the French, to whom the other redoubt had been assigned. With this dashing exploit Hamilton's military career came to an end, and

[1] See Appendix, Note B.

he soon after betook himself to the pursuits of civil life.

I have touched upon these incidents of Hamilton's army life because they throw a strong light upon his subsequent career, enable us to understand his course in aftertimes, and furnish the key to certain qualities which explain his thought and action. But there are other phases of mind and character suggested and exhibited by this eventful war period. Between his leaving the quiet college and the storm of the Yorktown redoubt, he was brought into close contact with many persons, and it thus becomes possible to study his capacity of dealing with other men, a matter of the first importance for any success in active life, and especially for a public man. In his position in the army there was no opportunity for so young a man to win general popularity, but this was something which Hamilton never attained, and indeed never sought. His genius and achievements were not of the kind which appeal to the hearts and imagination of the people ; he was too great a man ever to descend to the arts of a demagogue, and he was too definite a man ever to have that vague popularity which hangs about some persons without any assignable reason. But, at the same time, Hamilton had an extraordinary power of making friends, and this comes out strongly in his army

life. It was not merely that he won the respect
of men of character and ability; any man of
equal talents was sure to do that; but he gained
the affectionate devotion of men of that sort,
and attached them to him. He was evidently
very attractive, and must have possessed a great
charm of manners, address, and conversation.
But the real secret was that he loved his friends,
and so they loved him. We see this on every
side. All his comrades on the staff, and all the
officers, young and old, who knew him and were
not hostile to Washington, loved him, and were
proud of his talents. The same was true of the
young French officers, with whom he was much
thrown on account of his perfect command of
their language, a very rare accomplishment in
the colonies. From Lafayette down they all
liked Hamilton, and spoke to him and about him
with all the quick enthusiasm and lively affection of their race. In all this we see the germs
of the power which afterwards gave Hamilton
a personal following, much smaller than that of
many of our party leaders, but in proportion to
its numbers unequaled in our history for character, ability, and devotion combined.

Another question which grows out of this
period is that of Hamilton's military ability.
Whatever he did in the war of the Revolution
was well done, but a large part of his service

was rather political and diplomatic than military, and he was too young to have the largest opportunities. He proved himself a soldier of courage, dash, and coolness; he showed that he had both nerve and foresight, all very essential qualities, but he had no chance to show more than this. He certainly believed that he had in him the making of a great general, and his military temperament and aptitude for military affairs go far to confirm this belief. If he had had the opportunity, it may be safely said that he would have been a distinguished general, but whether he would have been a great one must necessarily remain a matter of mere conjecture.

Yet, whatever his talents for war may have been, the ruling passion was that of a statesman, and even in the midst of the hardships of the camp and field nothing could repress Hamilton's strong natural bent. Neither physical discomfort nor visions of military glory could keep him from meditating on questions of government and finance. At the beginning of 1780, being then just twenty-three years old, he addressed an anonymous letter to Robert Morris on the financial affairs of the Confederacy, at that time in their worst state, and threatening far more than the British armies to bring the Revolution to an untimely end. The paper begins with a careful consideration of the condition of the nearly worthless currency and the causes of its depreciation. It all looks very simple as we read it now, but at that time political economy was unknown, the modern systems of financiering were unheard of, and the true causes of financial phenomena were still hidden. Away from such books and authorities as there were, and relying on his memory for his facts, Hamilton gives an analysis and explanation of the depreciation of the currency admirable in its clearness and soundness, thoroughly modern in reasoning, and conclusive in argument. Young as he was, he allowed with singular penetration for the part which the imagination plays in all such matters as credit and currency, and reckoned on it as a factor with great exactness. This little essay on inflated and depreciated currency is as valuable to-day as when it was written a century ago, and proves beyond question an inborn genius for finance, showing its author indeed to be entitled to stand with Turgot and Pitt as a pioneer in what has since become the most important department of practical government. This remarkable essay was only preliminary. The youthful aide-de-camp had his remedy outlined in his head and ready for execution. He proposed to meet existing difficulties by gradual contraction, a tax in kind, and a foreign loan, which last was to form the basis of a national

bank.   The great purpose of the bank, and
indeed the pith of Hamilton's scheme, was to
unite the interests of the moneyed classes in the
support of the government credit.   The bank
was to be a great trading and banking corpora-
tion in private hands, but backed and partly
controlled by the government, to which it was to
be under certain obligations.   The details were
carefully worked out, but the leading ideas suf-
fice to show the grasp of Hamilton's mind and
the germs of his future policy.

A few months later Hamilton addressed a
letter to James Duane, then a member of Congress from New York, on the subject of the
government.   A large part of this document
is devoted to the army, then in sorry plight,
owing to the inefficiency of Congress and the
ill-adjusted relations of the States.   The root
of the evil Hamilton finds in the weakness of
the central government and the jarring and independent powers of the States.   He urges
stronger government, single men at the heads
of departments, and the absolute control by
Congress of certain functions, such as making
treaties, controlling the army and navy, and the
like.   To bring these things to pass, he says that
Congress must either resume the discretionary
powers which it exercised at the outset and then
suffered to decline, or else a convention must be

called to form a new, strong, and well-defined central government. Neither scheme was possible at that time, and the second, which was soon of course to be the true remedy, was at that moment of war and confusion more impracticable even than the first. The letter concludes with an outline of the bank as the best method of dealing with the most crying evils. The whole paper is strongly centralizing in tone, especially for that time, although Hamilton had not then got beyond thinking that senates were liable to become dangerously aristocratic.

A month later he writes a brief letter to the New York patriot, Isaac Sears, in which he sums up the results of his reflections as follows : —

"We must have a government with more power. We must have a tax in kind. We must have a foreign loan. We must have a bank on the true principles of a bank. We must have an administration distinct from Congress, and in the hands of single men under their orders. We must above all things have an army for the war, and an establishment that will interest the officers in the service."

Six months afterwards, in the spring of 1781, to Robert Morris, then at the head of the finances, he writes again, setting forth his scheme for a national bank with all the additions and improvements obtained by a year's reflection.

These letters are all interesting, not merely
because they display Hamilton's talents in the
strongest way, and show the breadth and scope
of his mind, but because they exhibit in the
clearest light the constructive character of his
intellect.   He was not only thinking like everybody else how the war could be brought to a
successful conclusion, and present difficulties
conquered, but also how a new system could be
built up on the ruins of the old fabric of society
and government.   His time had not come; the
world about him was occupied, as it always is,
with the immediate exigency; it had not even
finished the work of destruction, and was very
far from having cleared the ground and made
up its mind to build again.   Hamilton's ideas,
as those of far-seeing and brilliant men are apt
to be, were a little before their time.   But people were coming nearer to them every day, and
in a few years just such a man would be needed.
The beginning was indeed close at hand, for
Hamilton went from the army almost at once to
a stage where he had opportunity for his first
experiments, and could learn in a hard school
the immense task which lay before him of con-
verting his theories into practice and turning
his schemes into realities.

CHAPTER III

LAW AND POLITICS

In the midst of the war Hamilton had found time to fall in love. On his mission to Gates he met at Albany Miss Elizabeth Schuyler. The acquaintance thus begun was renewed in the following spring, and then ripened into an engagement. Late in the same year, on December 14, 1780, he was married. This was in every way a most fortunate event for Hamilton. He not only won a most charming and intelligent woman for his wife, but he allied himself with a family rich, well known, and of the best position in the community. His father-in-law, General Schuyler, a brave, generous, honest gentleman, was universally beloved and respected, and thus Hamilton secured the firm anchorage which his wandering fortunes needed. He was no longer an isolated stranger, as much at home in one state or city as in another, but a member of a strong family deeply rooted in their ancestral soil. On the other hand, Hamilton brought to this respectable and important Dutch family not only the society of an attractive man, but the

rising fortunes of one whose brilliant talents
had, as everybody could divine, a great destiny.
Certain it is, that he was most warmly received
by his wife's family, and the wide connection
thus formed by marriage was soon held by the
much stronger tie of personal friendship.

But whatever else Hamilton brought his wife,
worldly goods were not among his possessions.
Love of money was never one of his qualities,
and he had an abiding confidence in his own
capacity to earn at any time as much as he
needed, so that at the close of the war he found
himself with a wife and child and no resources
except his arrears of pay and his own abilities.
He steadfastly refused General Schuyler's generous offers of assistance, and betook himself at
once to a study of the law, the profession by
which he intended to get both fame and bread
and butter.   At the conclusion of a few months'
study, early in the summer of 1782, he was
admitted to the bar. His preparation was hasty,
and his knowledge, when he came to the bar,
must have been exceedingly imperfect, but with
his intensity of application and readiness of
mind he had undoubtedly gathered in that short
time a good deal of legal learning; and, what
was far more to the purpose, it was not an undigested mass of information, but was thoroughly
systematized and arranged. Everything that

Hamilton had in his mind, everything, certainly,
to which he gave his attention, took the shape
of argumentative statement. All his serious
ideas fell naturally into the forms of logic, and
with a little effort he could throw his thoughts
on any subject into numbered paragraphs, and
make them assume the guise of a concise brief.
In a word, Hamilton had, above all things, a
classifying and logical mind. His hasty legal
studies came, of course, within the operation of
this rule of mental action. As fast as he acquired his knowledge of law, it fell into well-
defined form and system, so that when he was
admitted to the bar all he had learned was com-
pactly stated and neatly arranged in a little
manual, which was found in manuscript by those
who came after him, and which, as we are told,
did good service to others whose minds did not
have a clarifying effect upon everything that
was poured into them.

But while Hamilton was studying law, and
even before he left the army, others, conscious
of his talents and feeling that he deserved well
of his country, had pressed him forward for
public office. He could have been a commissioner of the French loan, but, always generous,
he gave way in order that his friend Laurens
might go to Europe and rejoin his father, fresh
from imprisonment in the Tower. His name was

brought forward and talked about in connection
with the peace commission; and finally, in June,
1782, Robert Morris, who appreciated Hamilton's abilities, appointed him continental receiver
of taxes for New York. Vested with his new
authority, Hamilton betook himself to Pough-
keepsie, where the legislature was sitting, and
where his restless spirit soon became apparent.
First came a set of resolutions demanding a
new convention and a better union of the States.
This the legislature was induced to pass. Next
followed a clear and scientific plan of taxation
to replace the impotent and chaotic system then
existing, but this the legislature would not adopt.
Then appeared an address to the public creditors, letters to the governor, pertinacious appli-
cations to all branches of the government and
all members of it, and vigorous efforts to obtain
for the central government the tardy and sorely
needed supplies. The results of all this zealous
work were pitiful. Hamilton squeezed out a
few thousand pounds, and with these, and his
resolutions in favor of a new convention of the
States, he was fain to be content. His activity
bore fruit, however, in another direction. The
acquaintance he made and the impression he
produced resulted in his election by the legislature as a member of Congress, in which once
brilliant but now feeble body he took his seat in

November, 1782, having resigned his receivership a month before.

When Hamilton entered Congress, it had fallen far below that predecessor of 1774–75 which extorted the applause of Europe, and which probably had a higher average of ability than any legislative body of equal numbers of which anything is known. It had not, however, in 1782, reached that condition of utter decrepitude into which it subsequently sank, nor did it, as yet, enjoy the full measure of that popular contempt which subsequently became its portion. It still had among its members men of ability and force. Conspicuous among them was Madison, young, but prudent, sagacious and acute, warped somewhat by his Virginia notions, yet, withal, a statesman of a high order, and second in talent to Hamilton alone. There were a few others, such as Wilson, Clymer, Bland, Higginson, and Witherspoon, men of reputation, sense, and ability, who stand out from the crowd; but most of the members, although well-meaning, were wholly commonplace, and totally unable to deal with the grave problems which confronted them. The difficulties of the situation were, in truth, immense. It was a time of social and political chaos, of broken promises and unfulfilled hopes. The storms of war had at least filled the sails, but they had now ceased to blow, and the ship of state was lurching terribly in the heavy sea, and threatening at every moment to go to pieces. Hamilton had entered upon a broader field, but he found the same disheartening obstacles which he had encountered in New York increased in Congress thirteen fold, and to be overcome by a legislature which was utterly powerless. Young, enthusiastic, and full of ideas, he flung himself manfully into the struggle. He made himself deeply felt at once, produced such an impression that he was talked of as fitted for several of the most important offices, and left the stamp of his clear and powerful intellect on everything Congress attempted to do. But it was all in vain. His most desperate efforts were fruitless; for, bad as things were, the condition of the times was such that they could not get better until they had become much worse. Let us glance for a moment at the various tasks to which he put his hand, as they come before us inextricably interwoven in this year of his public service. They will serve to show the persistent energy and strong sense of the man, and the evil days on which he fell at the opening of his career of political action.

Just as Hamilton was entering Congress Franklin was engaged in the diplomatic campaign which ended in such a signal triumph for the American envoys. When the issue of

the negotiations became known in this country,
there were plenty of men ready to abuse the
astute old philosopher and his colleagues for
violating their instructions in proceeding without the coöperation of France, and for agree-
ing to a secret Florida article with the British
commissioners. The natural hatred of England
had been balanced by a trust in France equally
natural, but far more unreasonable. On this
principle Congress, with what amounted to pos-
itive servility, and guided by the subtle Luzerne, had placed the negotiation within French
control, and this was the command which the
commissioners had boldly and wisely disobeyed.
Hence the outcry from lovers of France and
haters of England. Hamilton, with his keen
insight and with the liberality of mind which
assured him that the envoys could judge better than he, was less extreme. Yet even he,
although soon to be stigmatized as "British,"
felt so favorably toward France, and so hostile
to England, that he advocated a middle course,
and introduced a resolution which, while it sustained and praised the envoys, provided, nevertheless, for the disclosure of the secret article
to the French minister. The signatures to the
preliminaries of the general peace cut the controversy short, but even at their worst our foreign relations were simplicity itself compared to
our domestic difficulties.

Finance was the overwhelming trouble which
laid bare the fatal vices of our political system,
and it was upon financial rocks that the rickety
Confederation was dashing itself to pieces. Our
affairs in the way of debts and taxation were
entering upon their last and worst phases at the
beginning of 1783, when the patriotic Morris
was resigning in disgust, and the young pro-
jector of national banks was new in Congress.
These were of course questions highly attractive
to Hamilton's genius, and therefore it was that
upon them his most strenuous efforts were wasted
while representing his State at Philadelphia.
The first object was to obtain consent to the
grant of an impost on imports. One State had
not been heard from, but Rhode Island was the
only one in active opposition, and to the conversion of this obstinate and selfish little community Hamilton addressed himself. He it was
who led the debate in Congress, who obtained
a committee to visit Rhode Island and argue
with their government, and from his pen proceeded a forcible letter to the governor. Even
while he was contending with Rhode Island,
Virginia receded from the agreement and the
whole scheme fell through. Had it succeeded,
it would, if the States had held to it, have furnished a permanent revenue, and hence Hamilton's zeal. Defeated at this point, Congress

fell back on its old policy of recommending a
grant for a term of years, and against this
Hamilton and Higginson voted with the Rhode
Islanders, who opposed all forms of taxation
or debt-paying. Hamilton explained his course
in a letter to Governor Clinton. He was not
willing to lend his support to schemes of proved
futility, or aid in the self-stultification of Congress, which progressed rapidly enough in any
event. The fact was that there were very few
adherents of what Hamilton calls " Continental
politics," which favored strong, honest measures
and the funding of the public debt. To this
the friends of the States made all possible opposition, and the result was helpless stagnation.
The government had no resources, for the only
one of any value, foreign loans, was nearly
exhausted. Hamilton looked with absolute disgust upon this dogged refusal to pay the price
of freedom, this stupid indifference to honor
rapidly degraded by the practical disregard of
all just claims, foreign and domestic.

But the blackest ingratitude, and the dishonesty which touched Hamilton most nearly,
was the treatment of the army, for Congress
contemplated disbanding these gallant soldiers
without even the pretense of providing for their
long arrears of pay. Washington regarded with
horror such an idea, and feared " most unhappy

disturbances." Hamilton had a notion that the
army might be used to threaten Congress sufficiently to induce them to make proper provision for all creditors; but Washington warned
him that the army suspected that it was to
be used for this purpose, merely to be thrown
aside afterwards, and that it was a dangerous
instrument to play with. Very soon this pre-
diction of possible disaster from men with arms
in their hands, and smarting with a sense of
wrong, came alarmingly near fulfillment, and
failed only through the influence of Washington himself. The army at Newburgh was in a
perilous condition, and the famous Newburgh
addresses show what might have happened if
Washington had chosen to put himself at the
head of the ill-used troops. But Washington
not merely refrained from uttering the fatal
word of ambition; he threw himself into the
breach, checked the whole movement, and quelled
so far as was possible the rising and dangerous
discontent. We hardly appreciate that at Newburgh Washington rendered one of his greatest
services. He did not put aside the crown, like
the Cæsar of Shakespeare, but the idea of sov-
ereignty never even entered his thoughts, never
for an instant darkened the unrivaled purity
of his utter unselfishness and single-minded-
ness. A word from him, and the star of the

Revolution might easily have gone down in
military rebellion and military despotism coming suddenly upon an exhausted and divided
country.   But all this Washington checked,
and the only outcome of the discontents was
a mutiny of some new levies near Philadelphia.
Even these mutineers, however, frightened the
feeble government, and produced a sharp controversy with the Pennsylvanian authorities, because they failed to call out the militia for
the protection of Congress, who thereupon employed Hamilton's vigorous pen to castigate the
lukewarm State.   In all these troubles Hamilton manfully took the part of the army, and
acted with the commander-in-chief.   He drew
resolutions of thanks to Washington, which
Congress readily adopted, for they were always
generous of fine words and empty phrases, but
the army got nothing.   They were sent unpaid
to their homes, taking their arms with them
as tokens of the gratitude of their country.
Hamilton urged the maintenance of a force
which should furnish the basis for future armies
if they were needed, but Congress cut it down
to the lowest point, retaining only some eighty
dangerous mercenaries in the national service.
Defeated at all points, Hamilton strove to have
the debates made public and the sessions open,
hoping in this way to exert the pressure of pub-

lic opinion, but he was once more flouted and voted down.

In the summer of 1783 Hamilton's term expired, and he withdrew to private life and to the practice of his profession. His congressional service had been a complete failure, so far as results were concerned. Even his iron energy of purpose had dashed itself in vain against the popular demoralization and indifference. The times were not yet ripe for the work he had to do. But, although he failed to accomplish anything for the good of the country, he extended his own reputation, and laid fast hold of a position which was sure to make him a leader in the future party of reconstruction. A letter from McHenry, written in October, 1783, gives in clumsy phrase a very exact idea of the effect produced by Hamilton in Congress. McHenry says : —

" The homilies you delivered in Congress are still recollected with pleasure. The impressions they made are in favor of your integrity ; and no one but believes you a man of honor and republican principles. Were you ten years older and twenty thousand pounds richer, there is no doubt but that you might obtain the suffrages of Congress for the highest office in their gift. You are supposed to possess various knowledge, useful, substantial, and ornamental. Your very grave, and your cautious, your men who measure others by the standard of their own creeping politics, think you sometimes intemperate but seldom visionary, and that, were you to pursue your object with as much cold perseverance as you do with ardor and argument, you would become irresistible. In a word, if you could submit to spend a whole life in dissecting a fly, you would be, in their opinion, one of the greatest men in the world. Bold designs; measures calculated for their rapid execution; a wisdom that would convince from its own weight; a project that would surprise the people into greater happiness without giving them an opportunity to view it and reject it; are not adapted to a council composed of discordant elements, or a people who have thirteen heads, each of which pays superstitious adorations to inferior divinities."

Besides reputation, Hamilton gained experience in Congress, and that of a kind which had a powerful influence on his opinions of politics and government. His mind was naturally conservative and order-loving, but he was also young and enthusiastic, and in the struggle with England he held very liberal views, was not only then as always a champion of constitutional liberty, but, in the days when he thought senates dangerously aristocratic, leaned strongly to democratic principles. These tendencies, developed by a war against oppression, were rudely nipped, first by the treatment of the gallant army of which he was a member, and

still more by his experience in Congress. The
natural impulses of his temperament once more
asserted themselves in all their strength. In
Congress, or rather in the States which were
there represented, he saw thirteen pure representative democracies, some of an extreme type.
The distinguishing qualities of these communi-
ties, and of the central government as well, were
at that moment faction, jealousy, and discord,
infirmity of purpose, feebleness in action, un-
blushing dishonesty in finance, black ingratitude toward the army, and the rapid acquisition
of an ever-growing contempt on the part of the
rest of mankind. The main difficulty lay clearly
in the overgrown rights of thirteen independent and jarring States. Next to this came the
inevitable disorganization and demoralization
consequent upon revolution, which Hamilton
saw plainly enough, but which he believed to be
deeply aggravated by too great an extension of
democratic principles. We can hardly wonder
that, constituted as he was, his conservatism
grew vigorously. From this period we may
date the conception of that aristocratic republic
and strong government, which was to be so
highly centralized that the obnoxious States of
the confederacy would sink to mere provinces,
and which found expression in the plan so eloquently presented by Hamilton to the conven-

tion of 1787. By the Congress of 1782–83
were planted, also, we may be sure, the germs
of that deep distrust of democracy and democratic systems which attained so great a growth
when it seemed to find in the French Revolution such awful confirmation. The one year of
Congress, utterly futile and barren as it seemed,
had a deep effect upon Hamilton; that is, upon
a man who was destined to leave a profound
impression upon the history of his country, and
who was to become the leader and type of a
powerful school of political thought.

Hamilton's withdrawal from public office was
by no means equivalent to separation from public affairs. Both as a lawyer in successful practice, and as a writer, he was a leader and mover
of opinion in New York. One of the great
troubles of the times was the popular attitude
toward the Tories, or loyalists, and in New York
the feeling was peculiarly bitter. There was an
active determination to take vengeance on all
who had sided with the crown and were now
helpless, and this was done in utter violation
not only of wise policy, of public morals, and
of the law of nations, but also in direct contra-
vention of the treaty with England. Hamilton
before leaving Congress had urged upon Governor Clinton the imperative duty of paying
British debts, as provided by the treaty, and on

his return to the bar he found himself at onor
engaged in a case growing out of these hostil
feelings. The legislature had passed an act,
known as the " Trespass Act," giving a right of
action to those whose property had been occupied during the war by loyalists. Relying on
this statute, a poor widow brought suit against
a rich loyalist merchant who had occupied her
property during the British ascendency. All
the sympathy and passion of the multitude were
with the plaintiff, but Hamilton, with the fine
disdain of popular clamor which always characterized him, took the brief for the defendant.
In a masterly argument, elaborate, eloquent,
and high-minded, he appealed to the pride of the
court to do justice, regardless of everything else ;
he reviewed every point of his opponent's case ;
raised the question from the narrow ground of a
wrongful statute and rested it on public morals,
the laws of nations, and the sanctity of treaties. He gained his cause, the first and one
of the greatest of the forensic triumphs which
gave him so high a place at the American bar,
and his victory was the signal for a burst of
legislative anger. The decision and the judges
were denounced, but Hamilton had stemmed the
tide, for the time at least, and, what was of far
greater importance, had led the court to vindicate its honor and sense of justice.

Other violent and revengeful acts against the loyalists followed, and the disregard of treaty rights gave England a readily-taken excuse for refusing to carry out her share of the provisions for indemnity and for the surrender of the posts. Again Hamilton came forward in behalf of a wise, liberal, and true policy of amnesty and conciliation. Snatching time from his professional labors, he sent forth two vigorous and widely read pamphlets advocating all that was just and statesmanlike in dealings with the loyalists and in observance of treaties. He remained unrefuted. Certain ones among his enemies planned to challenge him successively until he should fall in a duel, but though they were ready to face his pistol they could neither meet nor answer his arguments. They had the good sense to abandon this murderous scheme, and no challenge was sent, but the idea was a very pretty compliment to Hamilton's power as a writer.

In other directions Hamilton's ability and activity were equally manifest. He was one of the founders and principal originators of a state bank, which was of good service, and cut off the land bank scheme of Chancellor Livingston, just then fascinating the very untrustworthy lawgivers of the State. In the formation of the Society of the Cincinnati he took an active part, and was one of its best friends and guides in the tumult of attack with which it was received in that day of narrow views and ungrateful suspicion. Thus these years slipped away in busy usefulness, but Hamilton never lost sight of the necessary changes in the national system, watching, waiting, and striving, in company with the few leaders like Washington who thought "continentally," to create a proper public opinion and bring about a successful national movement.

CHAPTER IV

THE CONSTITUTION

1786–1789

WHILE Hamilton was thus engaged in the pursuit of his profession, taking an active part in many matters of general importance, and laboring with a chosen few for the education of the people in the right direction, and for the establishment of a national party, public affairs were rapidly going from bad to worse. The people, who had won the admiration of Europe in their conduct of the opposition to England and in the war for independence, had now become an object of general contempt, and were very nearly at the lowest stage of degradation in the eyes of the world. Divided among themselves, with no army, no navy, no cohesion, floundering willfully and helplessly in a sea of unpaid debts and broken promises, the States of the confederacy were bankrupt in money and reputation alike. The great powers looked on with gratification, each seeing a possible victim in America, and coveting a share of the spoils.

England, beaten in battle, and determined on
revenge if not redress, held the western posts,
kept the Indians in her control, and the borders
in a state of terror and ferment, while by hostile
proclamations and discriminating laws she sought
to ruin the commerce of her former colonies and
embroil them still further with each other.   To
France the Revolution had offered a splendid
opportunity to gratify the passionate longing for
revenge engendered by the terrible disasters in-
flicted by Pitt.   The ministry and the court of
Louis XVI. watched American affairs closely,
and when the moment of assured victory seemed
to have come, they gave us welcome aid.   They
intended to strike a terrible blow at England,
and they did it.   The fine gentlemen and gallant soldiers who came here came for vengeance.
If we except Lafayette, nearly every one in
France, from the king and his ministers down,
were animated by policy and revenge.   The sen-
timental sympathy of fashionable Paris would
have done but little for us.   Self-interest did a
great deal.   Having helped us most essentially,
and having at the same time used us for her own
purposes, France now aimed covertly to obtain
control of her former allies, and even Spain insulted and defied us.   The disintegration of the
general government was spreading to the individual States.   The future State of Kentucky

was breaking off from Virginia; Wyoming was
a sharp thorn in the side of Pennsylvania; New
York, at odds with Massachusetts, was still
more deeply embroiled with the settlers of what
was to be Vermont, and with New Hampshire.
As the States in their selfishness and blindness
trampled on the confederacy, they began to feel
the effects of this conduct in these disorders
within their own limits. The finances of every
State, with hardly an exception, were utterly
debauched. Fresh inflations of worthless currency were coupled with barbarous laws to enforce its circulation and compel its acceptance.
Public bankruptcy was followed by personal and
private distress, and then came stay-laws, and
every sort of dishonest expedient in the so-called
interest of the debtor class. In every State,
too, were local leaders, like George Clinton and
John Hancock, who saw in a strong central government a great diminution of their own consequence. They preferred being first in their
villages to being second at Rome, and therefore
headed, directed, and gave force to the ungov-
ernable majority, and gained political prosperity
from the evils of the time. The first sobering
shock came from Massachusetts. In that State,
one of the richest and strongest in the confederacy, the Shays rebellion broke out, threatening
courts and law with extinction. Hancock, the

popular hero, had prudently resigned, and James
Bowdoin, a man who thought "continentally,"
was left to crush the insurrection, and sacrifice
his popularity in the service of the State. The
whole affair was soon over, but it had its effect.
The miserable fabric of the central government
had tumbled at the stroke, and armed anarchy
and rebellion looked terribly unpleasant when
men were brought face to face with them. They
did more to arouse the people to a sense of their
desperate condition than all the brilliant reasoning of Hamilton or the great influence of Washington.

From Massachusetts, too, under the lead of
Bowdoin, came the first effort for a better union
in the form of instructions to her representatives
to urge the necessity of a new convention upon
Congress. But the representatives were chosen
by the states-rights party, for in truth there was
at that time no other, and they smothered the
instructions, explaining their course at their lei-
sure a twelvemonth later. The first attempt
had failed, but had done its share of the work
of drawing public attention to the true remedy
and its necessity. The successful movement
came from the commercial interests. Virginia
and many other States were striving for a retal-
iatory agreement against England, but nothing
could be effected. New York was particularly

selfish, and the neighboring States were beginning to open free ports and discriminate against New York and against each other. These warring and increasing jealousies were, of course, destroying our commerce and crippling the country. Virginia, having made a commercial convention with Maryland, was struck with the idea that it would be a good plan to extend it to the other States, and in a burst of liberal feeling passed resolutions in January, 1786, calling for a convention at Annapolis to consider the establishment of a uniform commercial system.

It is at this point that Hamilton's share in the formation of the Constitution begins. In this limited and unpromising opening he saw a chance to bring about a convention with powers great enough to reorganize the government throughout and save the sinking fortunes of the country. It was but a stepping-stone, and a small and slippery one at best, but, if properly used, the next stride might be to a gathering capable of extended and enduring work. With this great end in view, some of his friends and followers secured seats in the legislature; and while the Clintonians were magnifying their State and their leader and helping to plunge the wretched confederacy still deeper in the slough of impotency, the little band of Continentalists "went their whole strength" on representation at An-

napolis, and succeeded in obtaining the appointment of five commissioners, of whom Hamilton
was one. After the fashion of that feeble and
demoralized time, only two commissioners, Hamilton and Benson, went to Annapolis, where they
met the representatives of no more than four
other States, such was the public indifference
to anything of national importance. The little
meeting could do nothing for commerce or anything else, but it was able to issue an address
calling another convention where the delegates
should come with general powers, such as New
Jersey had given in the present instance. This
address was drafted by Hamilton, and after it
had been toned down to suit the sensibilities
of Virginia and of Edmund Randolph, governor
thereof, it was sent out to the people. In simple
and forcible terms it set forth the condition of
the country, the evils and dangers which threatened it, and the grave need of a complete reor-
ganization of the government. The little gathering at Annapolis had done its work, and played
its part as a stepping-stone. It now remained
to make the convention which was to come a
success.

With this end in view, Hamilton gained an
election to the legislature of New York, and at
once assumed the lead of the forces opposed to
the governor. He served on many important

committees, and took an influential part in all
the business of the House. The dividing question was the grant of a permanent revenue to
Congress. Here Hamilton had already been at
work and had written and distributed an address
to the people, denouncing the refusal of New
York to comply with the request of Congress.
The preceding legislature had granted the revenue, but under conditions which nullified the
act. Congress had asked for an extra session to
reconsider this action, and Clinton had refused.
In January, 1787, the new legislature was obliged
to meet the question. All reason and a great
deal of ability besides Hamilton's were with the
general government, but Clinton had the votes.
After a hot debate, the governor obtained an
approval of his course, and after a still more
protracted struggle, in which Hamilton shone
with the full lustre of eloquent argument, the
grant of the impost was defeated. Clinton and
his followers gave the finishing stroke to the
confederacy, completed its wreck, and left the
country to choose between anarchy and union
on a new basis. They builded better than they
knew.

But while Hamilton, with practical good sense,
was straining every nerve to sustain Congress
and give the existing system, wretched as it was,
another chance for life, he did not lose sight of

the grand object which he had kept in view for
years, and which had brought him to the New
York legislature. In the course of the session
his talents had been fully displayed, his personal
attraction had been deeply felt, so that despite
the hostile majority he carried through a resolution for the appointment of five delegates to the
coming convention. The Senate cut down the
number to three, and defeated a second resolution, which Hamilton carried in the House, to
add two more. The election of delegates followed, and resulted in the choice of Chief Justice Yates, John Lansing, Jr., and Alexander
Hamilton. Yates and Lansing were uncompro-
mising Clintonians and states-rights men, who
could be relied upon to vote against any form
of improved federal government. The fact of
their election is the best evidence of the odds
which Hamilton had overcome in securing the
resolution for their appointment. Notwithstanding the character of the delegates, Hamilton had
won a decided victory in the very teeth of a
compact majority by forcing New York to be
represented in the convention.

On the 25th of May, 1787, the representatives
of nine States were assembled at Philadelphia,
and the work of forming a new Constitution
began. It is no part of my purpose to enter
into the history of that famous convention.

Hamilton's great services to the cause of the
Union and the Constitution were rendered before and after its meeting. From the day when
he wrote from Washington's camp the letter to
Duane setting forth the scheme of a stronger
government, he had never ceased to labor for
that end. In every legislative body within his
reach he had striven for resolutions commend-
ing that object. He it was who had seized
with quick sagacity on the opening afforded at
Annapolis and turned it to such good account.
He had labored incessantly to form public opinion by essays in the newspapers, by addresses
and speeches, while in private letters he kept
up constant communication with those leaders
who thought as he did, and sought always to
make converts where his words or his friendship
could have weight. By great sacrifice of time
and by strenuous exertions he had forced New
York to appear at the convention, and had
toiled to gain the approbation of Congress for
the new enterprise. At last his thought and
labor were near fruition. The convention which
he had urged had met, he was himself a member, and yet he still stood alone, master only of
his own personal influence. In the decision of
the momentous questions he was helpless, for
the vote of New York was in the hands of his
enemies and sure to be cast against him on

every occasion. To have contested every position with his colleagues, and at every trial to
have voted against his State, would only have
impaired his standing and injured his cause.
He therefore prudently refrained from the useless and unequal conflict, took comparatively
little part in the debates on details of the Constitution, and was absent a large part of the
time from the convention. In conversation with
the members he could persuade and counsel, and
this he did; but he wisely decided to concentrate
all his force in debate in one speech. For this
purpose he selected at the beginning of the convention, after the various plans had been submitted, the general theme of a new government.
Completely master of his subject, filled with a
deep conviction of the solemnity of the occasion, he delivered a speech occupying five or six
hours, described by Gouverneur Morris as the
ablest and most impressive he ever heard, and
embodying all the accumulated reflections of
years. The brief remains to us, and in that
bare outline can be readily traced the range and
variety of the speech. He spoke of the gravity
of the occasion, of the choice possible to the
convention; he reviewed the whole science and
theory of government, and, with an overflowing
abundance of illustration, surveyed the entire
domain of historic precedents; he showed our

low condition, the evils of the existing system, and the resulting principles on which a new government should be founded. Delivered with all Hamilton's impressive energy, glowing with the ardor of the speaker, and expressed in language at once forcible and transparently clear, we may well believe that this speech had a profound effect.

In the course of his argument he read his own plan for the new government, carefully worked out and perfected. This plan, which discloses the essence of his opinions on government, followed in a general way the English system, as did all others presented, including the one finally adopted. In after times Hamilton was severely reproached with having said that the British government was the "best model in existence." In 1787 this was a mere truism. However much the men of that day differed, they were all agreed in despising and distrusting *a priori* constitutions and ideally perfect governments, fresh from the brains of visionary enthusiasts, such as sprang up rankly in the soil of the French Revolution. The convention of 1787 was composed of very able public men of the English-speaking race. They took the system of free government with which they had been familiar, improved it, adapted it to the circumstances with which they had to deal, and put it into successful operation. Hamilton's plan, then, like the others, was on the British model, and it did not differ essentially in details from that finally adopted. But it embodied two ideas which were its cardinal features, and which went to the very heart of the whole matter. The republic of Hamilton was to be an aristocratic as distinguished from a democratic republic, and the power of the separate States was to be effectually crippled. The first object was attained by committing the choice of the President and senators, who were to hold office during good behavior, to a class of the community qualified to vote by the possession of a certain amount of real property. The second was secured by giving to the President of the United States the appointment of the governors of the various States, who were to have a veto on all state legislation. These provisions, as may be seen at a glance, involved the essential character of the government, and although purely republican, came much nearer to the British model than any other by their recognition of classes and of the political rights of property, while by the treatment of the States a highly centralized national government was to supersede entirely the confederate form. In the Congress of the Confederation, Hamilton had seen that all the difficulties arose from the too great power of

the States, and further, as he believed, from the
democratic form of their governments. With
his usual bold decision, therefore, he struck at
the root of the evils and struck hard. Many of
the states-rights men in the convention dreaded
too much democracy, when applied to the people
of the United States collectively, but they were
far from approving the vigorous ideas of Hamilton. The majority of the members undoubtedly favored a democratic system in the Union,
such as they were familiar with in their own
States. Even those who believed with Hamilton, that in the best government there should be
an infusion of aristocracy, had no disposition to
risk what was then deemed the last chance for a
respectable union, on a scheme which would be
hopeless of acceptance. There can be no doubt
that Hamilton, with his keen perception of existing facts, was perfectly aware that the leading
principles of his plan stood no chance of adoption, either by the people or the convention.
The aim of his great speech and of his draft of
a constitution was to brace the minds of his
fellow members and to stimulate them to taking
higher ground than the majority of their con-
stituents demanded. In this he succeeded. His
eloquent reasoning, if it did not lead men to
his own conclusions, at least raised their tone,
enlightened many members, and brought them

to a more advanced ground than they were at
first prepared to take. This was all of great importance, and to work for such results was, in
Hamilton's isolated position, his wisest course.

His message once delivered, he waited and
watched, aiding quietly and effectively whenever
he could, but not attempting to thrust himself
forward, fettered as he was by the action of his
own State. His colleagues, however, abandoned
the convention, and at the close Hamilton, not
shrinking from the responsibility of representing alone a State where opinions adverse to
his own prevailed, once more took part in the
debates and affixed his name and that of New
York to the Constitution. When the end was
thus finally reached, he sprang once more to
the front and gave free rein to all his activity
and zeal. It was in this last decisive struggle,
in securing the acceptance of the work of the
convention, that Hamilton rendered his greatest
services to the cause of the Constitution, — services more important and more effective than
those of any other one man at this last stage
of what was in truth a great political revolution.

I have said that Hamilton had no expecta-
tion of the adoption of his own plan of government by the convention, but he none the less
thoroughly believed in it. He thought it bet-

ter and more enduring than the one actually
adopted, and he never lost faith in its principles. Indeed, as the distrust of democracy
disclosed in his plan by the proposition for an
Executive and Senate to be chosen by a qualified suffrage grew and strengthened in the conflicts arising from the French Revolution, Hamilton's confidence in his own theory deepened,
and his faith in the existing Constitution declined. But when the work was complete at
Philadelphia, when he had put his name to the
compromise which he had anticipated, and in
which he rejoiced, he gave his loyal adherence
to the new Constitution and the new system.
Had he been an agitator, or a sentimentalist of
muddy morals and high purposes, a visionary
and an idealist, he would have stood up and
howled against this Constitution, which was not
what he wanted, and which fell so far short of
his own standard. As he was none of these
things, but a patriotic man of clear and practical mind, he knew that the first rule of successful and beneficial statesmanship was not to sulk
because one cannot have just what one wants,
but to take the best thing obtainable, and sustain it to the uttermost. In the Constitution,
however imperfect he might think it, he saw a
vast improvement and unlimited possibilities,
and for the adoption and successful working of

the Constitution he prepared to labor with all his strength.

In the country at large, and in most of the States, there was a majority against the Constitution, but there it was before them, and the people had to make their choice between that and anarchy. They did not see the alternative quite so plainly as we do now, but that they felt it is shown by the fact that, while a large majority longed to say "No," a very narrow majority in eleven States did say "Yes." The choice thus forced upon the people by the submission of the Constitution did away almost everywhere with the miserable indifference which had become the prevailing sentiment in regard to all things national. Parties began to spring up, the press teemed with controversial essays and letters; and more emphatic marks of interest, in the shape of rioting and burning in effigy, were not wanting.

New York was not the most important of the States, either in wealth or population. In these respects she was surpassed by Virginia, Massachusetts, and Pennsylvania, and her adhesion to the new scheme was considered much less vital than theirs. But in geographical position, capable as she was of dividing New England from the Middle and Southern States, New York had great importance, and almost made

up in this way what she lacked in wealth and
population. Her assent to the new scheme thus
became of great moment, and it was very difficult to gain. In New York party feeling had
always run higher than elsewhere, and it was
now extremely bitter. The opposition there to
the new Constitution was stronger, more compact, and better led, and had a more active,
powerful, and unscrupulous chief, than in any
other State. In the city of New York a society
was formed to resist the adoption of the Constitution by the state convention; and there, very
soon after its signature, a concerted attempt
was made in the Clintonian interest to write
down the new scheme in a series of connected
and well-planned essays. This was a gage of
battle which Hamilton was ready enough to
take up. He asked nothing better than to debate the question before the tribunal of public
opinion. The challenge was promptly accepted,
and the reply came in the form of a letter
signed "Publius," written in the cabin of a little vessel as Hamilton was gliding quietly down
the tranquil current of the Hudson River. The
work thus begun extended over many weeks, a
new number appearing, as a rule, every three
days. In the midst of the most pressing avo-
cations, both public and professional, Hamilton
always found a moment in which to turn his

ready pen to the vindication of the Constitution,
so that the series might never be interrupted.
In this great work he was much assisted by
Madison and slightly by Jay, both of whom
brought ability, training, and sound sense to
the task. There has been some controversy as
to the proportionate share of these eminent
men in this undertaking, but the discussion is
of little moment. The original conception was
Hamilton's, he wrote considerably more than
half the numbers, and to posterity "Publius"
will always be Hamilton. This remarkable
series of essays, famous as "The Federalist," is
still the best exposition of the Constitution apart
from judicial interpretation. "The Federalist,"
throughout the length and breadth of the United
States, did more than anything else that was
either written or spoken to secure the adoption
of the new scheme; but it was something more
far-reaching than a timely and practical piece
of argument. The countless pamphlets, essays,
disquisitions, and letters which saw the light
at the same time have disappeared. They
have been consigned to the dust-heaps of history, and the waters of oblivion have rolled
over them. But "The Federalist" still stands.
No one will deny that it is dry, and that it is
not calculated to amuse an idle hour, but the
"Oceana," the "Leviathan," the "Fragment on

Government," are not easy reading, and yet they are intellectual possessions highly prized and not to be parted with. As an exposition of the meaning and purposes of the Constitution, "The Federalist" is now and always will be cited on the bench and at the bar by American commentators, and by all writers on constitutional law. As a treatise on the principles of federal government it still stands at the head, and has been turned to as an authority by the leading minds of Germany intent on the formation of the Germanic empire. In a word, "The Federalist" marks an epoch in the development of free constitutional government, in the art of confederation, and in political thought. On these essays Hamilton's fame as a writer has always rested and must always rest, although many of his other political papers are of equal ability and force.

The immediate results of "The Federalist" were so important that its literary merits have been somewhat overlooked. These essays have, in fact, become so firmly imbedded in our political history that their place in our literature has been forgotten. The development of colonial literature was rudely arrested by the troubles with England and by the conflict of the Revolution, when the intellectual force of the community was wholly absorbed by politics and war. After the peace, constitutional and political questions, and the struggle for material prosperity, engaged exclusively the mental energies of the people. The result was that we had absolutely no literature except the literature of politics. This presented, of course, a very restricted field, and literature of this sort, that is, literature with an object and as a means to an end instead of one cultivated purely for its own sake, can never be of the highest order. In this single branch, however, the standard was very high. The genius of the people in this direction was strong and keen, and their faculties had been sharpened still further by the long controversy with the mother country, in which the talent displayed by the arguments of the colonists upon constitutional points and the ability of the American state papers had extorted the admiration of the leading minds of England. It may be safely said that in dealing with questions of politics and government the people of the United States were second to no other nation. When a man entered the arena of political discussion he not only encountered vigorous opponents and competitors, but he appealed to a public whose judgment on these particular subjects was highly trained. In this literature the essays of " The Federalist " take the first place. They exhibit a wide range of information ; their reasoning is strong; their style is simple, forcible, and clear; they were admirably adapted to their purpose; and above all they have endured, for they were a fresh and original contribution to human knowledge and to the best thought of the time. The conception of "The Federalist," and the lion's share of the essays, belong to Hamilton, and entitle him to the first place in the literature of the day. This is especially true if we take "The Federalist" in connection with his other writings in various forms and at different times, but always upon kindred topics. Hamilton has won in this way an important position in the literary history of America. It may be fairly said that his work takes the first rank in the only literature of the time. When it is remembered that he was also a busy lawyer, an active politician, and a great statesman, this is high praise, even if the literature in which he was foremost was nothing more than the literature of politics.

By the publication of "The Federalist" Hamilton rendered his first preëminent service to the adoption of the Constitution; his second was by securing the adhesion of New York. Clinton had failed to prevent the call of a state convention by the legislature, where the Federalists prevailed after a sharp struggle; but now that the last decisive conflict was upon him, he gathered all his forces and prepared for battle.

He triumphed without serious trouble in the
election of delegates, and found himself master
of forty-six out of sixty-five votes when the convention, which chose him to be their president,
assembled. The Clintonian majority was led by
Melancton Smith, a keen debater and a man
of ability, and by Yates and Lansing, Hamilton's
colleagues at Philadelphia. The slender minority of nineteen was headed by Hamilton, ably
supported by Jay and Livingston. " Two thirds
of the convention and four sevenths of the people
are against us," wrote Hamilton, as he surveyed
the unpleasing prospect, anxious and grave,
but full of courage. The outlook was in truth
disheartening ; but we may well imagine that
Hamilton felt instinctively the coming victory,
that he rejoiced like the strong man to run the
race, hopeless as it seemed, and that he prized
the laurels to be won all the more on account
of the odds which confronted him and the hard
fight which must be fought. The first issue
was on postponement. The Clintonians urged
delay, in order to see the experiment tried, to be
guided by the other States, to examine further
the scheme, and so on with all the excuses of
procrastination. Their ground was shrewdly
chosen, but the Federalists met the issue boldly,
and when it came to a vote, even the devoted
partisans of the governor shrank from settling

the momentous question by evasion, and postponement was defeated. Then the work of the Philadelphia convention was taken up, sharply debated, and minutely scrutinized in every clause and paragraph. Day after day Hamilton was on his feet upholding the cause of the Constitution. Every opinion which he had expressed was turned and twisted into a weapon of personal attack, and he was constantly assailed as if he and the Constitution were one. Defending and explaining his own position without weakening his cause, he debated every point and met his vigorous opponents in constant battle. No detail was too small to be dealt with, no flight was too distant for him to take. Filled with his subject, thoroughly familiar with all that could be said on both sides, he reasoned and pleaded, exhausting every resource of argument. When the Constitution had been thus reviewed, it could be seen how his work had told. The opposing forces faced each other for some days in complete inaction. The Clintonians, despite their majority, dreaded to come to a direct vote, uncertain as to the precise effect of Hamilton's arguments. The Federalists, who had been fighting for time and knew that time was working with them, were in no haste to move. Nine States had ratified. The experiment would surely be tried, and presently came the news

that Virginia had assented. The old policy of
evasion was once more attempted by moving an
adjournment, and was again defeated. Then
came a long string of amendments and a proposal for conditional ratification. Hamilton met
this in a brilliant speech, and Melancton Smith
confessed that conditional ratification was absurd. The end was near. A short interval
elapsed, and then Melancton Smith admitted
that he had been convinced by Hamilton, and
that he should vote for the Constitution. This
was the signal for a break, and when the vote
was taken the Constitution had a majority of
three in its favor. Bearing with him these joy-
ful tidings, Hamilton hastened to take his seat
in Congress, to which he had been elected some
months before despite a vindictive opposition on
the part of the governor.

This New York convention was an epoch in
Hamilton's life. It so chanced that in the years
which remained to him he had no opportunity
after this to take part in a great debate. His
eloquence found vent repeatedly, of course, at
the bar and in public meetings, but never again
in convention or in Congress. Thus it happens
that his legislative career closed when he was
barely thirty, and yet he had attained the very
first rank as a parliamentary orator. This fact
is as rare as it is remarkable, for high position

of this sort is usually the crown of a life spent
in legislative debate. Hamilton's case is an
almost solitary instance of a man's achieving
this difficult reputation while the work which
was to stamp him as one of the great legislators
and statesmen of his country still lay before
him. This sounds like mere panegyric, but a
little consideration shows that it is only the
simple truth. Hamilton's victory in securing
New York came at a time when the land was
filled with debate and discussion; when besides
the national convention at Philadelphia there
were twelve state conventions, and when all the
talent of the nation was called into conspicuous action. That under such circumstances one
state convention should be obscured is hardly
to be wondered at, and thus the magnitude of
Hamilton's success simply as an achievement
of parliamentary skill and eloquence has been
lost sight of. In New York the difficulties were
greater than elsewhere. The hardest struggles
in other States were in the two great common-
wealths of Massachusetts and Virginia. In the
former, however, all the ability of the State was
banded together to sustain the Constitution; by
skillful tactics, Samuel Adams and John Hancock, the great leaders of the states-rights party,
were disarmed and partially converted, so that
those who confronted the Federalists in actual

conflict were very inferior men. In Virginia
the ability was pretty equally divided between
the contending parties, but the opposition was
much less stubborn and unreasonable than in
New York or Massachusetts, while the Federalists had the inestimable advantage of Washington's enormous personal influence. In New
York, if we exclude Hamilton, the preponder-
ance of ability was with the governor, who in
political strength and management was a host
in himself. The majority against the Constitution was very large, carefully disciplined and
counted, compact, and ably led. This majority Hamilton overcame by open debate. He
changed votes by his untiring succession of brilliant speeches, and when party lines are drawn
there is nothing so rare as such a feat in all the
long records of parliamentary contests. He did
this, too, in the midst of continued personal
attacks, which he was compelled not only to
ward off, but to keep distinct from his cause.
It is true that circumstances worked with him,
but this was part of his campaign; and that the
pressure caused by the accession of other States
was not necessarily decisive is shown by the postponement of the question in North Carolina and
the refusal to call a convention in Rhode Island.
Any one familiar with legislative bodies and
with parliamentary history can appreciate the

meaning and weight of the confession wrung
from the leader of the majority, when he admitted that he had been convinced by Hamilton on
a question which had agitated the public mind
for months, and on which party feeling had run
high. Tried by the severest test, that of winning votes, Hamilton's victory is of the highest
rank in the annals of modern oratory.

That the new States were almost painfully
deficient in nearly everything which gave refinement to the Old World civilization — in art,
in literature, in philosophy, in social splendor —
cannot be doubted; but in politics, constitutions
of government, and public law they were more
advanced than any other people; and in capacity and skill in parliamentary debate and political controversy they were as well versed and as
keen as their brethren of the House of Commons. In this field, therefore, Hamilton can be
measured by standards as high as any then in
existence, and can be compared with any of his
contemporaries on either side of the water. His
many speeches have perished, for there were
no shorthand reporters; he spoke extempora-
neously from the stores of an overflowing mind,
and only meagre outlines of arguments and
striking sentences condensed to the last point
remain. Yet it is not difficult to analyze the
qualities which made Hamilton a great orator.

Concerning the intrinsic merit of what he said,
there is no need to go farther than the essays
of "The Federalist" to learn that they were
profound expositions of the principles of constitutional law and of the state of public affairs.
In the same essays, or in any other of Hamilton's pamphlets or reports, we can also find
that he set forth his ideas with wonderful clearness, directness, and force, often with intense
compression, at times with a great variety of
illustration. All these attributes avail much
to clear men's minds of error and to convince
them of truth. But behind the lucid reasoning
and the nervous expression there must have
been something more, — some qualities which
moved men's hearts. Inconceivable as it seems
with such topics, we yet know from eye-witnesses that Hamilton moved his hearers to
tears. What was it that could do this? To
stir an indiscriminate crowd to tempests of grief
or rage is not an uncommon power; to move to
deep emotion a legislative body, in this instance, of course, largely hostile and made up
of picked men, is an extraordinary feat. From
Hamilton's letters and essays, — indeed, from
everything he ever wrote, — we know that he
was not a man of strong or fertile imagination.
He would never have pictured a coalition by
describing the junction of the Rhone and Saone

with a felicity of expression which was startling
in its vivid exactness, or held his hearers breathless as he drew the fanciful retrospect of the
aged Bathurst. In a period when tropes, meta-
phors, and images were fashionable, Hamilton
dealt but little in them. With him, thoughts
and sentences are alike simple, strong, and
straightforward, and these he used effectively
and convincingly, not by delighting the imagination and beguiling the fancy, but by commu-
nicating through his words, voice, and manner
his own spirit. That he had pathos, sympathy,
and depth of feeling can be seen in the André
letters, and these qualities did him good service; but that which led him to victory was
the passionate energy of his nature, his absorp-
tion in his work, his contagious and persuasive
enthusiasm. He rises before us from the past
small in stature, but erect and graceful, and by
the art of the chisel and the brush we can see
the firm, strong jaw, noble head, long, straight
nose, and, most effective of all, the dark, deep-
set eyes. We can easily imagine how he looked,
with his eyes glowing and flashing as he became excited, and how his full, melodious voice
rang out, compelling the attention of all who
listened.

Hamilton's speeches in the New York convention do not live on the lips of schoolboys.

They suffered from having been spoken in a
small state convention at a time when eleven
other similar assemblies were held. They had
none of the splendor which came to Pitt and
Burke from their forum; none of the glitter of
the gorgeous pageant which gathered in West-
minster Hall to listen to the wrongs of the Be-
gums; none of the national lustre which encir-
cled Ames when he shook Congress with dread
at the prospect of war with England, or Clay
when he denounced the Essex junto, or Webster when he upheld the cause of the Union.
Yet if we try Hamilton's speeches by the severest tests, by the conversion he wrought, by
the sustained power, the readiness, fertility, and
resource he displayed, and above all by results,
this series of speeches in the New York convention deserves to rank with the highest triumphs
of modern parliamentary oratory. Such at least
was the opinion of his contemporaries, both
friends and foes. In the grand procession by
which the Federalists of New York celebrated
their victory, the federal frigate was named the
" Hamilton," while the opponents of the Constitution assailed him for using such consummate
art in oratory that he blinded, hoodwinked,
and misled his hearers, preventing their voting
in accordance with their real convictions, so
bewitched were they by the magic of his words.

No greater compliment could have been paid
him; and when his bitterest enemies ranked his
eloquence so highly, posterity may fitly adjudge
its place to be among the first.

The great battle had been fought and won,
but much remained to be done. The demands
of New York and Virginia for a new convention to amend the Constitution must be evaded,
and officers of the new government who were
sound Federalists must be chosen. Hamilton
carried through Congress the ordinance fixing
the dates and the place for putting the new
government in operation, and then turned his
attention to New York. His reward was defeat
for reëlection for the unexpired term of the old
Congress. Clinton, though beaten, held his
men together in an extraordinary way, and
with an unyielding grasp. The Federalists controlled the Senate, but Clinton had the House
when the New York legislature assembled. The
result was an obstinate dead-lock, and New
York was unrepresented in the first electoral
colleges, and had no senators when the new
Congress met. The state elections soon followed, and Hamilton flung himself heart and
soul into the campaign. Yates was nominated
by the Federalists, as a moderate man able to
draw votes from the other side, and Hamilton
supported him eagerly and eloquently with voice

and pen in the newspapers and on the platform.
This choice of a candidate was due to Hamilton,
and it may well be doubted whether he would
not have done better if he had nominated some
steady Federalist.   He would certainly have
strengthened his party, but he was probably
led to select Yates by the desire to win at
all hazards.   His hatred of Clinton probably
blinded his judgment, which, whenever it went
astray, was warped by the energy of his personal feelings.   At all events, the doughty governor prevailed once more, despite the exertions
of his enemies, but his power was broken.   His
majority was a very narrow one, and the legislature was in favor of the Constitution.   This
gave the senators to the Federalists, and by
most desperate efforts they succeeded in choosing four of the six representatives in Congress.

The election of the senators was marked by
one of those errors into which Hamilton was
led on one or two memorable occasions by his
imperious will and headstrong disposition.   Up
to this time the Livingstons, one of the ruling
families in New York, had acted with and given
powerful aid to the friends of the Constitution.
They cheerfully conceded one senatorship to
Schuyler, but they and others like Morgan
Lewis desired the other, as it is said, for some
New York man of their faction, and they were

especially opposed to King, whom Hamilton
had settled upon as Schuyler's colleague.[1] Rufus King was an eminent and able man, but he
had just come from Massachusetts, and could
not in the nature of things have had any following of his own. Hamilton, nevertheless, persisted, and King was chosen. The result was
a rupture with the Livingstons, which was the
probable cause of the defeat of Schuyler two
years later, and of the election of Burr. King
was no doubt an abler man than any of his
competitors, but the Livingston alliance was
very important to the Federalists, and it was a
blunder to throw it away. Hamilton had, in
fact, no genius for management, and his beset-
ting danger was in his desire to force things
through, and in his impatience of delay or of
concession, when dealing with other men. In
this case his imprudence brought strength to
Burr, and was the beginning of Hamilton's
many troubles in New York politics.

Meanwhile the day had come, the eventful
4th of March, fixed for the assembling of the
new Congress. The evil habits of the old confederacy still clung to national affairs to such
a degree that a quorum of both houses was not
obtained until April 6. Then the votes were
opened and counted, and George Washington

[1] Morgan Lewis to Hamilton, June 24, 1789, MS. letter.

was declared to be President by a unanimous vote; and John Adams, who had received the next highest number, obtained the Vice-Presidency. Washington and Adams, on being informed of their election, proceeded by slow stages to New York, where they were sworn in and the government was fairly organized. The great experiment was at last on trial.

CHAPTER V

ALTHOUGH early spring saw the actual formation of the government of the United States, it was not until September 2 that the act passed establishing the Treasury Department. All eyes were turned to Hamilton as the man to fill this great office. Washington had already decided upon him, and Robert Morris had singled him out as the statesman suited above all others for the trying position which he himself had filled under the confederacy. Advisers were not wanting, tried friends and admirers, like Troup and Gouverneur Morris, who warned Hamilton of the trials he was about to encounter, and of the thorny path he must tread. They had reason enough on their side. Despite his politics, Hamilton, benefiting like other young patriots by the law excluding Tories from practice in the courts, had raised himself to a leading position at the bar, and had wealth and reputation within easy reach. All this quiet and assured prosperity must be sacrificed for a post beset with difficulties, of unceasing toil,

and with a paltry salary of thirty-five hundred
dollars a year.   There is, however, no indication
that Hamilton wavered for a moment in his
decision.   He was convinced that he could render his best service to his country at the head
of the Treasury, and he at once accepted the
high office.   It could not have been otherwise.
His time had come, the great epoch of his life,
and it was impossible to escape his destiny.
He was only thirty-two years old, in the flower
of his age and with the flush of youth upon him.
The weapons which he had been forging for
years hung at last complete and glittering before
his eyes, and he was the last man to refuse to
gird on the sword and draw it in the cause of
good government.

Ten days after Hamilton's appointment Congress directed him to prepare a report upon
the public credit, but this order, which led to
the development of his whole financial policy,
was only one of the many tasks allotted to him.
It is not a little amusing to note how eagerly
Congress, which had been ably and honestly
struggling with the revenue, with commerce,
and with a thousand details, fettered in all
things by the awkwardness inherent in a legislative body, turned for relief to the new secretary. They knew Hamilton's reputation and his
perfect familiarity with theories of finance and

government, and they seem to have felt instinctively that he was a great minister of state with a well-defined policy for every exigency. In the course of a year he was asked to report, and did report, with full details, upon the raising, management, and collection of the revenue, including a scheme for revenue cutters; as to estimates of income and expenditure; as to the temporary regulation of the chaotic currency; as to navigation laws and the regulation of the coasting trade, after thorough consideration of a heap of undigested statistics; as to the post-office, for which he drafted a bill; as to the purchase of West Point; on the great question of public lands and a uniform system of managing them; and upon all claims against the government. Rapidly and effectively the secretary dealt with all these matters, besides drawing up as a voluntary suggestion a scheme for a judicial system. But in addition to all this multiplicity of business there were other matters, like the temporary regulation of the currency, requiring peremptory settlement. Money had to be found for the immediate and pressing wants of the new government before any system had been or could be adopted, and the only resources were the empty treasury and broken credit of the old confederacy. By one ingenious expedient or another, sometimes by

pledging his own credit, Hamilton got together
what was absolutely needful, and without a mur-
mur conquered these petty troubles at the very
time when he was elaborating and devising a
far-reaching policy. Then the whole financial
machine of the Treasury Department, and a system of accounting, demanded instant attention.
These intricate problems were solved at once,
the machine constructed, and the system of
accounts devised and put in operation; and so
well were these difficult tasks performed that
they still subsist, developing and growing with
the nation, but at bottom the original arrangements of Hamilton. These complicated questions, answered so rapidly and yet so accurately
in the first weeks of confusion incident to the
establishment of a new government, show a
familiarity and preparation as well as a readiness of mind of a most unusual kind. Yet
while Hamilton was engaged in all this bewildering work, he was evolving the great financial policy at once broad, comprehensive, and
minute, and after the recess in January he laid
his ground plan before Congress in his first
report upon the public credit, a state paper
which marks an era in American history, and
by which the massive corner-stone, from which
the great structure of the federal government
has risen, was securely laid.

It was with this report that Hamilton entered
upon the most important part of his career, and
at the same time upon the period in which he
impressed his individuality strongly upon the
history and development of the United States.
The first report on the public credit was not
only the beginning of a remarkable financial
scheme which achieved a brilliant practical success, but with its successors which came quickly
after it, from the fertile mind at the head of
the Treasury, it carried out a far-reaching policy
which affected, as it came to maturity, the character of the whole government, built up and
welded together a powerful party, and founded
a school of political thought which still endures
and has always exercised a profound influence
on our material growth and our political and
constitutional system. Up to this time, great
and valuable as Hamilton's services had been,
they were simply those of a man of remarkable
ability, having no peculiar mark about them.
The intellect and personality of Hamilton have
not left their stamp and superscription upon the
Constitution as it went from the Philadelphia
convention, but upon the government, the public policy, the political system which grew up
under the Constitution, they made an indelible
impression in those early and plastic years, and
one which has never been effaced. In a word,

when Hamilton sent in his report on the public
credit in January, 1790, from being a distinguished man he became also a typical leader,
and, most important of all, an essential element
in our history.

To attempt to give an abstract of this report
would be labor wasted. With all his lucidity of
statement, Hamilton was always concise, especially in his communications to Congress, and
to such a degree that further condensation is
out of the question. But to understand Hamilton and his influence as a great factor at the
dawn of the history of the United States, it is
sufficient to lay bare the main principles of his
report. In these we can obtain the intent and
significance of his policy, and then compare it
with its results. After setting forth in general
but striking terms the necessity of public credit,
not merely as a means of raising money, but as
an element of national greatness, and after
dwelling on the need of the most rigid honor
in all things connected with financial dealings,
Hamilton states in a few curt sentences the
objects to be attained. He says : —

"To justify and preserve the confidence of the
most enlightened friends of good government; to promote the increasing respectability of the American
name; to answer the calls of justice; to restore landed
property to its due value; to furnish new resources

both to agriculture and commerce; *to cement more closely the union of the States;* to add to their security against foreign attack; *to establish public order on the basis of an upright and liberal policy;* — these are the great and invaluable ends to be secured by a proper and adequate provision, at the present period, for the support of public credit."

I have italicized the two sentences which seem to me to embody the most essential points of the whole policy. The cardinal doctrines of Hamilton, in questions of politics and government, were strength and order. The more intimate union of the States, effected by a common interest in the solvency and maintenance of a common government, was a sure instrument to promote strength. This was plain and is plainly stated, but the general expression, " to establish public order on the basis of an upright and liberal policy," covers, whether intentionally or not, a world of meaning, which finds explanation in the whole course of Hamilton's career and of his political thought. Public order usually is the condition precedent of sound finances. Here it is made the consequence. By the regulation of the finances, not only the strength of the government was to be increased, but public order was to be established. It was, in truth, the old idea which held a leading place in Hamilton's youthful scheme of a bank,

of building up a strong party in support of the
government. This was not merely to invigorate an existing political party or to evolve a
new one, although such a result was incidental,
important, and expected. Hamilton's scheme
went farther, seeking to create a strong and, so
far as was possible and judicious, a permanent
class all over the country, without regard to existing political affiliations, but bound to the
government as a government, by the strongest
of all ties, immediate and personal pecuniary
interest. The wisdom of this was obvious, when
the object was to sustain a great experiment;
yet at the same time Hamilton's purpose was
not simply by the spread of a popular loan to
unite a numerous body of men in the support
of the government, but chiefly and mainly to
bring to his side a class already in existence,
that which controlled the capital of the country.
The full intent of the policy was to array property on the side of the government. That
once done, the experiment, Hamilton felt, would
succeed, and its powers, moreover, might then
be much extended. He had been unable to
introduce a class influence into the Constitution
by limiting the suffrage for the President and
Senate with a property qualification, but by
his financial policy he could bind the existing
class of wealthy men, comprising at that day

the aristocracy bequeathed by provincial times
to the new system, and thus, if at all, assure to
the property of the country a powerful influence
upon the government.

The method by which these great ends were
to be reached, as well as the others, hardly
less important, which are also set forth in the
sentence quoted above, was by funding and con-
solidating all the debts of the United States
incurred in the war or growing out of it. The
most immediate practical gain which Hamilton
promised himself in this was, that the funds
would supply that deficiency of a circulating
medium under which the country labored, and
this point he argued at length and with great
ability. He proposed several schemes for funding, comprising various forms of annuities and
of payment in order to attract all classes of
creditors. Into these financial details it is not
necessary to enter. To fund the whole debt at
the existing rates of interest, he believed to be
beyond the power of the country at that moment; and in view of the great improvement to
be effected, and the appreciation of the debt
which had already taken place, he demanded
present concessions from the creditors. To use
a modern phrase, he offered long bonds at a low
rate of interest, four per cent., and short bonds
at six per cent. He proposed to pay two thirds

of the debt in the new funds, to bear interest at once, and the remainder in land, or in funds which should bear the same rates of interest at some future time. The propositions were honorable and practicable, and involved ultimate full payment, so that, to creditors who had generally begun to regard their loans as hopelessly lost, they must have seemed positively brilliant. Hamilton further proposed a sinking fund, which was to be made up at the outset from a new loan of ten millions placed in the hands of commissioners for the purchase of certain classes of the debt, and for otherwise facilitating the financial operation of the government, and which was also to be the receptacle of all savings and surplus, and thus provide for the accumulation of the means necessary to meet and extinguish the debt as it became due. This was nothing more than the ordinary sinking fund, as it is used and understood at the present day, not only in all civilized governments, but in innumerable corporations. It was merely a means to provide for actual savings to be applied to the extinction of debt. But coming at a time when Pitt was using " sinking fund " as a term to conjure with, and by ingenious calculations of the rates of interest was perfecting a juggle which served to blind a whole generation of Englishmen, and which actually led them to

believe that debts could be extinguished, not
by payment, but by further borrowing, this arrangement is interesting from its business-like
simplicity and sense. There was nothing of
Pitt's ingenuity about Hamilton's plan. To
him the sinking fund was a convenient business
device; nothing more. He had too keen a
mind to be deceived himself, and he had no
wish to confuse and befool others. His financial schemes were to be truthful and genuine,
if nothing else; and he put forth his scheme of
funding and sinking, not as the incantation of
an enchanter, by which debts could be paid without saving, but as business-like arrangements
by which honor could be restored, honesty and
reputation retrieved, the nation strengthened,
and the debt, so long as the necessary evil of
its existence endured, become, by taking on a
new form, a blessing instead of a curse to the
business interests and moral tone of the whole
country.

Such, in brief outline, were the objects at
which Hamilton aimed, and the means by which
he hoped to compass them. Nothing remained
but to determine the subject-matter to be dealt
with; and here came the crucial question of
what constituted the debt of the United States.
Few men questioned the value of the purposes
set forth by Hamilton, for on the surface, and

in most cases from any point of view, they com-
mended themselves to the hearty support of
all sensible men. There were few, too, who
objected to Hamilton's mode of funding; although at a later time in his career, and also
since it has all passed into history, there has
been some hostile criticism on this point, which I
shall refer to again. But as to what constituted
the debt, there were immediate, wide, and bitter
differences of opinion resulting in the first great
political struggle of the United States, and lay-
ing deep and solid foundations of party divi-
sions. Hamilton divided the debt into three
parts : the foreign debt, the domestic debt, and
the debts of the States incurred in the cause of
the Union during the war of the Revolution.
All these together amounted in round numbers
to above eighty millions, — hardly more than
Mr. Sherman saved in a twelvemonth in the interest account of the United States, but a very
terrible sum in the year 1790. Every one was
agreed about the foreign debt; every one was
likewise agreed as to paying the domestic debt,
but there were wide differences as to how and
to whom this latter payment should be made.
These two classes covered about fifty-four millions of the debt; and then came the state
debts, amounting to twenty-five millions, very
unevenly distributed, bristling with opposing

interests, the great bone of contention, and a subject of long and sore conflict. Thus the work was mapped out, and Hamilton concluded his report with estimates of ways and means, a scheme for raising revenue by duties on teas, wines, and spirits, and in the background a plan for an excise.

Before discussing the fate of this great report and its momentous political results, it is best to review briefly the other reports which followed close upon it, and were in reality parts of one comprehensive scheme. In this way the whole broad financial policy of Hamilton comes into view, and all the causes being thus understood and grouped together, it becomes far easier to appreciate the effects upon the country and upon its history.

The assumption of the state debts made an increase of revenue absolutely necessary, and at the close of the year 1790 Hamilton took the next step in perfecting his policy by sending to Congress his second report on the public credit, urging the establishment of an excise which he had already suggested, but which had been laid aside. Some additions he showed could be made to the duties imposed, but these were insufficient, and it became necessary to raise revenue elsewhere. Hamilton's general theory was to have as little direct taxation as possible, and to raise

as much revenue from articles of luxury as was
consistent with successful collection. Having
carried the duties on imports as high as he felt
they would bear, he turned naturally to the domestic manufacture of spirits as the best and
most proper resource. No one now will question that by all the best principles of political
economy Hamilton was right in his choice, and
that he selected the most appropriate subject for
taxation. The revenue being essential, this was
the least burdensome way to raise it, and the subject was one which in its nature should always
be taxed before anything else, and as heavily as
it will bear. On economic principles, the excise on spirits suggested by Hamilton requires
neither explanation nor defense. The real difficulty was political, not economical. It was true
that excises had been laid and collected by several of the States without objection. Hamilton
in fact cited these precedents, but to the popular
mind they were not precedents at all, for the
people did not try taxation by the States according to the principles which they applied in judg-
ing of taxation by the general government. An
excise laid by the States was like all other taxes;
an excise laid by the general government met in
the popular feeling the famous definition given
to it by Dr. Johnson. The attempt to raise
an internal revenue had led to the Revolution.

The government of England was external, and
the consequent hatred of government of that
description, combined with states-rights, had
proved the ruin of the Confederation, and was
the greatest menace to the new Union. The
old confederate government had laid or had
attempted to lay duties; the new government
was formed for that purpose, and to the customs
which everybody expected there was no objection. But although the right of the central government under the Constitution to lay an excise
was perfectly clear, it seemed to come from an
external government; it was new and unexpected, and was calculated to rekindle the slum-
bering animosity against anything resembling
external power, and to revive all the old jealousy
of the states-rights party. All this Hamilton
saw plainly enough. He endeavored to disarm
opposition by a careful diminution of the hated
powers of the officers of the excise, taking from
them their usual summary jurisdiction and carefully limiting their right of search. But if he
was cautious, he was also determined. Revenue
was necessary, and an excise on spirits was the
best resource from an economical point of view.
Moreover, the secretary was bent on vindicating
the right of the government to collect an internal revenue. It was an important assertion of
power, and one which ought to be at the com-

mand of the government, and which if once carried into successful practice would be another
element of strength. It was part of the general
scheme, economical and political; it was a bold
and perhaps a perilous move leading to grave
consequences, but Hamilton made it unflinch-
ingly, and then turned all his energies to securing its successful operation.

The day after that which gave date to the excise report saw the report on the national bank
transmitted to the House of Representatives.
This report embodied in an elaborated and perfected form the fruit of Hamilton's earliest
meditations on finance in the dark days of the
war. In a national bank he then saw the surest
staff to aid the tottering steps of the young and
struggling republic; and now, in the plenitude
of his power at the head of the Treasury and
of a vigorous party, he turned to it as a fundamental element of a broad and national financial
policy. The report was an elaborate essay on
national banks with a full display of their advantages, forcible replies to all the anticipated
and usual objections, and a clear but detailed
plan of the bank which the secretary wished
Congress to establish. The late Earl of Bea-
consfield once announced that it was necessary to educate his party; and in a similar
fashion Hamilton began his report by confessing

that he wished to educate the public, and that
this must be his excuse for such a lengthy pre-
sentation of a subject so simple and so familiar
to the "superior information" of the Congress
he addressed. Putting ourselves, in the wisdom
of our day and generation, on the same plane
as that which Hamilton's friends in Congress
occupied a century ago, we can lay aside the
educational details and arguments on banks and
banking. These same details and arguments are
admirably arranged and most lucidly expressed;
they were full of instruction then; it is not impossible that they might be of value in that way
even to the present enlightened age; but still
they are at bottom argumentative and instructive, and are far from easy reading. They do
not help us particularly to appreciate the character, influence, and meaning in history of the
man who wrote them down, so we may fairly
dispense with them here, and confine ourselves
to the great principles of the report as an essential part of a broad general scheme.

The plan of the bank was a good one, practical and successful; but that, too, is not of
importance here. The bank was to have the
support of the government, and the government
was to have the use of the funds, and to a certain extent and in a last resort the control of the
bank. The objects to be attained were in the

main the same as those aimed at by the funding
system. The economical problem which confronted the United States was how to develop
their vast material resources. The difficulty lay
in injured credit, both public and private, in
lack of capital and circulating medium, and in
the almost complete deficiency of the financial
machinery necessary to the conduct of domestic
trade and foreign commerce. In a national bank
Hamilton perceived the means of restoring general confidence, so important to large and remu-
nerative business transactions. In the issue of
bank notes he saw a large addition to the circulating medium of the country, and a great
expansion of credit. These notes would have
all the strength imparted by the close alliance
between the bank and the government, without
the dangerous qualities inherent in irredeemable
government paper. Facilities for exchange and
for the transaction of business throughout the
States, not merely for the government in the
collection of taxes and in all its other dealings,
but for individuals everywhere, would be pro-
moted to a degree which we can hardly conceive
without picturing to ourselves a community almost utterly destitute of all the appliances by
which the vast concerns of the business world
are now kept in daily motion. All these great
benefits flowing from the national bank were

correct in theory, and proved equally so in practice. They were all sought by Hamilton for the
great purpose of advancing the development of
the resources of the country, which, economically
speaking, was the pole-star of his whole financial
policy. They were intended to facilitate trade,
encourage enterprise, enhance the value of land,
and stimulate at once and as strongly as possible
both agriculture and commerce.

In the bank, too, there was also a valuable
engine for the performance of the financial work
of the Treasury, and a fresh source of power and
strength to the government. In the same manner as the funds, the bank would create a class,
or call forth one already in existence in support
of the government. The stockholders of the
bank would be even more united and more active than the holders of the funds, because they
would have more to gain. Then, too, in addition
to this powerful body of allies, the government
would find in the resources of the bank a great
assistance in time of distress, and a uniform system of finance and of bank notes everywhere
receivable would replace the chaos of thirteen
jarring States, each with its own banks issuing
notes which were universally distrusted beyond
their own borders. The power and purposes
of a national bank were seen as plainly by
Hamilton's opponents as by his friends, but its

immense economical value and necessary usefulness prevailed. The policy of a national bank
thus founded by Hamilton has never been per-
manently laid aside. When the charter of the
first expired, the very party, and some of the
very men even who had most fiercely resisted it,
established another. A few years later, and the
president of the national bank struggled with
the President of the United States on not unequal terms, a curious verification of the power
which Hamilton believed he should find in a
bank, and of the possible danger of that power
if arrayed against the government, as predicted
by Hamilton's opponents. Then came an inter-
regnum of state banks, and again difficulty and
distress led to a return to Hamilton's policy.
The system of national banks has replaced the
Bank of the United States and its branches,
doing away with the danger of extreme centralization in a single institution, which would be at
the present time of perilous magnitude. But
though the form has been thus wisely changed,
the policy of national banking and the gov-
erning principles are still those laid down by
Hamilton, and we live now under the sound,
wise policy in this respect which he devised and
carried through nearly a century ago.

But there is another side still to Hamilton's
plan of a national bank, which overshadows

all its other purposes and results, important
and far-reaching as they were. This was the
constitutional side. The opposition denied the
right of the government of the United States to
erect a national bank, and Hamilton evoked
the implied powers of the Constitution to bring
him victory. The struggle went into the cabinet, and Hamilton's argument not only satisfied Washington, but has carried conviction to
a majority of the American people ever since.
This argument on the constitutionality of the
national bank, as a piece of legal reasoning,
is the most important which Hamilton ever
produced, not only in itself but because it can
be tried by the highest possible standard. In
McCulloch v. Maryland, Chief Justice Marshall
went over precisely the same ground on the
same question, deciding the point, as is well
known, in Hamilton's favor. There are few
arguments which will bear to be placed side by
side with those of Marshall, but Hamilton's
stands the comparison without suffering in the
trial. The able and luminous decision of the
chief justice adds nothing to the argument of
the secretary and takes nothing from it, nor is
the work of the latter inferior to the opinion
of the judge in clearness and force of expression. I am far from meaning to imply by this
that Hamilton was as a lawyer the equal of

Marshall, who stands at the head of all lawyers, especially on constitutional questions. But it may be truly said that a man who could in much haste produce an argument which can be placed beside an opinion of the great chief justice, involving the very same question, is fairly entitled to stand in the front rank of lawyers, and can be credited with the possession of legal talents of the highest order.

Interesting as this comparison is to the student of Hamilton's life and character, the historical weight and meaning of the argument lies in the calling into vigorous life the implied powers of the Constitution. This great doctrine, embodying the principle of liberal construction, was the most formidable weapon in the armory of the Constitution; and when Hamilton grasped it he knew, and his opponents felt, that here was something capable of conferring on the federal government powers of almost any extent. Beside the doctrine of the implied powers, all the other schemes of Hamilton to give strength to the new system, far-reaching and striking as they were, sank into insignificance. Hamilton did not shrink. Strength, order, and national force were his objects, and in the implied powers he could find everything that he needed, or that the government could need, provided his progress was not arrested.

On the doctrine thus boldly laid down as to the bank, great parties have arisen and divided ever since, and a large part of our history, constitutional and political, has turned on the implied powers first seized by Hamilton. The growth of nationality and the conversion of the agreement of thirteen States into the charter of a nation have been largely the development of the implied powers. This is the central point of Hamilton's whole policy, and in his bold declaration of the implied powers of the Constitution he laid bare his one predominant purpose of building up a powerful national government.

In a little more than a month after the transmission of the report on the national bank, the indefatigable secretary of the treasury sent to Congress his report on the establishment of the mint. This was of course an integral part of his financial policy; but it was purely financial, and had none of the wide political and constitutional importance which attaches to the other reports. This essay on coinage, for such it really was, shows all Hamilton's thoroughness of treatment and clearness of thought and expression, applied to an intricate and difficult series of questions. The most interesting feature of the report to us lies in Hamilton's advocacy of a double standard. His argument was moderate in tone; he fully admitted the necessity of conforming in this matter to the practice of other countries and of the commercial world, and especially of England, with whom we had our largest dealings. He also frankly admitted the difficulties attendant on maintaining a proper ratio between the metals, so that one by being overvalued should not drive the other out. But after all deductions, and with full allowance for all possible risks, he comes clearly to the conclusion that in the long run greater steadiness is acquired by maintaining a double rather than a single standard, and that a better circulating medium, larger, more convenient, and less subject to dangerous fluctuations, is thus attained. This principle was adopted at the time, and with a short interval has been the policy of our government ever since. We now depart from the views expressed by Hamilton with reference to a double standard by disregarding our relations on this point with our principal customers and by grossly overvaluing the inferior metal.

In discussing the subject of coinage Hamilton advised the decimal system, with the dollar as a unit. He examined minutely the intricate details of alloy, gave a full plan for the working force and organization of a mint, and explained a careful scheme for coining and for

the methods and charges of the government in
this work. The report as a whole is of interest
merely as showing Hamilton's knowledge and
industry in every branch of finance, and the
general soundness of his views, which in this instance have been in the main closely followed
ever since.

Some months later, at the close of this same
year 1791, Hamilton put the finishing touch to
his financial policy by his report on manufactures, the most elaborate, and economically the
most important, of all his reports, and at the
same time the most far-reaching politically. It
rested on the implied powers of the Constitution, and was intended to do more than anything else toward the development of the resources of the country, the purpose nearest
Hamilton's heart, and toward rendering the
nation as strong and independent materially
as in all other ways.

That Hamilton looked for immediate results
from his report on manufactures may well be
doubted. He certainly knew that progress
would be deliberate and growth slow in this
direction. But he wished to sow the seed, to
prepare the way and lay down the lines to be
followed, and so much he did. From Hamilton's report on manufactures have sprung the
protectionist policy and the so-called "Ameri-

can" system of Clay. Hamilton was in his
grave many years before protection was seriously taken up as a well-defined system, but
when it came, stimulated, it is true, by the mistaken acts of his great opponent, it came as
he had foreseen it would come, and it succeeded as he had wished it to succeed. Upon
the principles then laid down, and upon the policy then boldly sketched with a master hand,
parties have divided and a great economical
system has been built up. Even after a hasty
examination, we can see in this paper, better than anywhere else, the grasp, and at the
same time the long reach, of Hamilton's mind
and thought. He was familiar with the science
of political economy, then in its infancy, and
with the writings of Adam Smith, the founder
of that science, whom he admired and quoted,
but whom he did not follow. The first pages
of the report are occupied with a brief discussion of the comparative value of agriculture and
commerce. The arguments of those who give
unquestioned preference to the former are met
and refuted, and the conclusion is that these
two pursuits are at least of equal value, that
they serve each other, and that it is best that
both should flourish. He then sets forth under
seven heads the advantages to be gained from
the establishment of manufactures, — division of

labor, extension of the use of machinery, additional employment to classes of the community not ordinarily engaged in business, promotion of immigration, greater scope for the diversity of talents and disposition which discriminate men from each other, a more ample and various field for enterprise, and the creation in some instances of a new, and in all of a more certain and steady, demand for the surplus products of the soil. The first objection is that a state thinly settled, with unbounded opportunities for agriculture, and able to buy manufactured articles from other nations, attains in this natural way the best and most profitable division of labor. To this Hamilton replies : " If the system of perfect liberty to industry and commerce were the prevailing system of nations, the arguments which dissuade a country in the predicament of the United States from the zealous pursuit of manufactures would doubtless have great force. . . . But the system which has been mentioned is far from characterizing the general policy of nations. The prevalent one has been regulated by an opposite spirit. . . . In such a position of things the United States cannot exchange with Europe on equal terms. . . . Remarks of this kind are not made in the spirit of complaint. . . . It is for the United States to consider by what means they can

render themselves least dependent on the combinations, right or wrong, of foreign policy."

The objection that industry if left to itself
will find out the most useful and profitable employment, and therefore should not be forced
by government, he meets by pointing out the
strong influence of habit and of the spirit of
imitation, including " the fear of want of success
in untried enterprises, the intrinsic difficulties
of first essays, and the bounties, premiums, and
other artificial encouragements with which foreign nations second the exertions of their own
citizens." He discusses this at length, taking
substantially the same ground as Mill in his
" Political Economy," that protection for nascent industries in order to remove the obstacles of starting is wise and proper. He then
examines at length the practical difficulties of
scarcity of hands, high wages, and want of capital, showing that the first two are exaggerated,
and need not be seriously injurious, and that
the third can be overcome by improved credit,
the expansion of the circulating medium by the
funds, and through attracting foreign capital.
To the objection that protection tends to create
monopolies and benefit a class at the expense of
the rest of the community, he replies, first, that
the increase of the price of commodities, even at
the outset, is much exaggerated, and does not

always occur; and, second, that in the end the
establishment of manufactures is a benefit and
profit to all. The same reasoning applies to
the objection that one section of the country
is aided at the expense of a loss to the other.
In the aggregate and ultimately, all must benefit, and agriculture will probably be directly
stimulated, as in the case of cotton, for which
manufactories in the North will at once open a
market. Then are shown the benefits to trade
from diversity of pursuits and product; and,
lastly, the wealth, and above all the independence and security, to be gained by manufactures.
In the vast territory of the United States almost
everything can be produced, and in the successful establishment of manufactures Hamilton saw
the road to an absolute independence far beyond
the reach of foreign nations.

With patient detail all important articles of
industry are examined separately, every small
advantage or disadvantage weighed and pointed
out, and every form of protection and govern-
mental aid carefully discussed. In the latter
are included premiums on invention and a
patent system, while a strong plea is made in
favor of assistance from the government in the
construction of roads and bridges. Here Hamilton introduces the doctrine of internal improvements, destined to be for so long a time a

subject of division ; and for this, as for protection, he finds his constitutional authority in the
theory of the implied powers, and in the broad
expression of the right " to provide for the general welfare." His plan for the encouragement
and establishment of manufactures was by a
combination of bounties and protective duties,
the surplus revenue of the latter to supply the
funds for the former.

In the year 1791, with all nations protecting
their manufactures, Hamilton was a strong protectionist, aiming chiefly at the development of
nascent industries. What he would be to-day
must be matter of speculation, but it is safe to
say that in the presence of the great results of
his policy he would not be likely to abandon it.
The report on manufactures, as it stands, contains the best and soundest argument, not on
the general question of free trade and protection, but on that question as connected with
the United States. " Most general theories,
however," says Hamilton at the outset, with
reference to free trade, " admit of numerous ex-
ceptions," and therefore he confines himself to
the United States, and has little to do with
abstract theory, except by way of respectful
mention. Hamilton's report, as an argument in
favor of protection, must be tried solely with
reference to the Uuited States, under all the

circumstances surrounding them, and with all their opportunities and possibilities. If it is put to this test, setting aside all its literary and scientific merits, it remains the best and most complete argument for a protective policy in the United States which we possess. No new and fundamental principle has been added to Hamilton's reasoning, but his report has been a welcome armory to generations of disputants, and is still waiting to be successfully answered and overthrown.

The report on manufactures completed the financial policy devised and carried through by Hamilton and the Federalists. During his official term he sent to Congress, of course, very many reports besides those which are here discussed; but in these four, indeed in three of them, his policy in all essential points is embodied. From these reports came the funding system, the revenue system, the sinking fund, national banking, the currency, and the first enunciation of the protective policy. They carried with them the great doctrine of the implied powers of the Constitution, and opened up the important question of internal improvements. So far as public policy could do it, they laid the foundation of the material prosperity of the United States. As Gouverneur Morris said, what was left of the Revolution grounded on finance, and so finance was the first all-absorbing and all-important question which confronted the new government of 1789. A successful financial policy meant the successful establishment of the new government. Behind all this lay the great constitutional doctrines which Hamilton raised up and defended, and the still greater political influence of his work. Hamilton was striving for a vigorous national life, and his chief object was to impart to the central government the greatest possible strength. He armed the government with credit and with a productive revenue; he won for it the hearty good-will of the business world; he gave it a potent ally in the national bank; by the funding system and the bank he drew out and welded together, with the strong influence of pecuniary interest, a powerful class, which knew no state lines; and by his protective policy and internal improvements he aimed to create yet another vigorous body of supporters, and give the government still more strength and popularity. It was a great policy, the work of a master-mind looking far into the future. It was the foundation of a great party, and the corner-stone from which the federal government was built up. It only remains to trace its history and results, as it was gradually unfolded before Congress and the people, and became the central point of politics and parties.

CHAPTER VI

THE publication of the first report on the public credit was awaited with intense eagerness. When it came, there was, of course, much excitement and a general rise in the securities of the bankrupt Confederation. Eager speculators hurried over the country to buy up the debt, and the secretary of the treasury already began to be regarded as one who could make the fortune not only of the government but of individuals. Congress having decided that they would not listen to the perilous oratory of Hamilton, but confine him to writing, took up the report. As to the payment of the foreign debt, all were agreed, and that portion was adopted without discussion; but on the payment of the domestic debt a fierce conflict arose. The root of this opposition was in the old repudiating, disintegrating spirit of the Confederation which still survived, and which found even plainer expression in resistance to Hamilton's proposition to pay the arrears of interest in the same way as all other indebtedness.

No one, however, was ready to take this stand against the domestic debt and advocate its absolute repudiation; perhaps, indeed, no one really desired such a proceeding in its fullest extent, although the old demoralization was really at the bottom of the hostility. The opposition sought to thwart the secretary and maim his plans, on grounds in appearance more reasonable and certainly more likely to arouse popular sympathy. They found their opening in the speculation which had begun with the adoption of the Constitution, and which reached a fever heat on the publication of the secretary's report, when the certificates of debt had bounded up to high prices at a single jump. The obvious cry was against the greedy and successful speculator in possession of the certificates, which he had obtained for a song from the original holders. The "original holder" now figured as a patriot cruelly wronged, and in many instances he was a soldier, which gave an additional point to the lamentations in his behalf, raised generally by men who, under the old Confederation, which still held their affections, had flouted with utter indifference all claims, both of soldier and patriotic lender.

But this inconsistency did not affect the value of the argument as a political cry. And there was, too, some ground for it in many cases of undoubted hardship. Hamilton and his friends freely admitted the force of this objection, but the secretary argued that the great object was to restore the credit and good name of the United States, to do what was just in the majority of instances and to the greatest number, and he urged, in conclusion, that any other course was impracticable. His reasoning could not be answered, but it did not quell the conflict. One proposition was, in cases where the certificate was in the hands of a purchaser, to pay him only what he had himself paid the original holder. The violation of contracts thus involved was the fatal objection of Hamilton ; but this plan carried with it, moreover, a very deep mark of the lurking desire to get out of debt by partial repudiation. To the surprise of every one, Madison came out in favor of discrimination ; but he admitted that the certificates must be paid in full ; and proposed a plan for a division between the original holder and the purchaser so hopelessly impracticable, that he could muster only thirteen votes in his support. Madison shrank from anything like dishonesty, but he was beginning to break from the friends of the Constitution and from the party to which he naturally belonged, because he felt the drift of Virginian sentiment, and was not strong enough to withstand the pressure. In this struggle, the supporters of the secretary, known as the Federalists, and hitherto acting merely as friends of the Constitution, first gained real cohesion as a party devoted to a given policy. Their only opponent of ability was Madison, and his opposition was rendered abortive and impracticable by his honesty and logic. The debate was long and heated, but the Federalists, having ability, sound reason, and the advantage of position on their side, prevailed. They also carried through the payment of the arrears of interest. Only one point remained, and that was the crucial test, the assumption of the state debts. Much had been done before this point was reached. Even if Congress went no farther than they had already gone, the credit of the country was reasonably safe; but the policy of the secretary would have been sadly mutilated. Public credit would not be rounded and complete; and, above all, the financial policy would have been deprived of much of its political and constitutional effects upon parties, upon the strength of the government, and upon the relations of the States. Sharp as the battle had been over discrimination in the payment of the domestic debt, it was a mere preliminary skirmish compared to the conflict upon assumption. The lines were clearly drawn, for Hamilton himself had marked them out. Parties were marshaled now, not on the acceptance of the Constitution, but as to the policy of the government created by the Constitution; and on the question of assumption they faced each other for the first vigorous, well-defined political contest in the history of the United States.

There was no need here to cast about for popular arguments, as in the case of the domestic debt, where the real grounds and objects of opposition were not clearly conceived, or were better hidden from view. There was an abundance of subsidiary and obvious arguments brought forward to the effect that too great a burden would be laid upon the people; that the state debts could not with justice be saddled upon the United States; that assumption was unfair in benefiting some States largely and not helping others, and among them some of the most deserving, at all. All these points were raised, and local feeling ran very high, particularly upon the last, leading to much angry recrimination and comparison of services in the Revolution. But after all was said, the most vigorous attack was against the chief purpose of the secretary, the end which he here had in view above all others of strengthening the national government by this large increase of its creditors, transferring the interest of a powerful class from the States to the Union, and in this way binding the States closer together and weakening enormously the vigor of the state-rights sentiments. Politically it was a bold and masterly stroke, but Hamilton's opponents saw at what it aimed as plainly as he did himself. A loud cry went up against this centralizing movement. The anti-Federalists, with reviving dislike of the Constitution, felt with sudden keenness the strength and pressure of the bonds which the minister of finance was drawing closer and closer about the people and the States, and they struggled desperately to get free.

Hamilton had foreseen this opposition, but he had reckoned on certain forces to sustain him, and he did not reckon in vain. His first ally was the enthusiasm aroused by his own policy; his second, the confidence and interest of the capitalists and merchants; his third, the direct pecuniary gain to certain States in the success of assumption; and his fourth and most important, the powerful body of able men in and out of Congress who desired a strong central government, whose objects were the same as his own, and who had found in him a leader about whom they could gather in solid phalanx. These forces prevailed. After a long and heated conflict, assumption was carried in committee of the whole, but the majority, although compact and

unyielding, was narrow. Delay served the opposition well. When the resolutions got out of
committee and came up in the House, the members from North Carolina, at last in the Union,
had taken their seats, and they turned the scale
against assumption. By their aid the resolution
was recommitted, and the Federalists, determined to have all or nothing, sent the rest of
the measures back with it. Again the party
opposed to assumption prevailed, and the whole
policy was at a stand. Feeling ran very high,
and ugly murmurs of dissolution began to be
heard. It looked as if the measures, destined
above all others to consolidate the new Union,
would wreck it at the very start. Hamilton
had summoned his spirits, and they had come to
him. All the forces he had calculated upon had
responded and done their work, but a new factor had been introduced and they could do no
more. The dead-lock was as perilous as it was
unforeseen, but the adverse majority was very
small, only two votes, and Hamilton was not
only determined but fertile in resources. He
would not yield one jot of his financial policy,
but he was perfectly ready to give up something
else; and in the site of the new capital, the
federal city, he found a suitable victim for the
sacrifice.

This matter of the seat of government had

excited great controversy and feeling between
States and sections.   Whether the future capital should be in New York or Pennsylvania, in
Virginia or Maryland; whether this inestimable
boon should fall to the North or to the South,
was a burning question second only to assumption.   Local prejudice and local pride were
raised to white heat on this momentous issue.
To Hamilton all this was supremely indifferent.
Much of his strength and somewhat of his
weakness as a public man came from the fact
that, while he was purely and intensely national
in opinion, and was devotedly attached to the
United States, he was utterly devoid of local
feeling and of state pride.   There is no evidence
that he cared one whit, except as a matter of
mere abstract convenience, where Congress fixed
the site of the federal city; but he was keenly
alive to the fact that everybody about him cared
a great deal, and whether reasonably or not was
of no consequence.   The party which favored
assumption were, as a rule, on the side of a
northern capital, and had prevailed.   The party
which resisted assumption favored a southern
capital, and had been beaten.   To gain the
necessary votes for assumption Hamilton determined to sacrifice what he justly thought was
a perfectly trivial question, and thus save the
financial policy which he rightly considered to

be of vital importance, and the very corner-stone of the new government. To carry out this scheme he needed the alliance of a Southern leader, and he pitched upon the man fated to become his great opponent, — the leader and type of one school of thought and politics, as Hamilton was himself the leader and type of the other.

Thomas Jefferson had just returned from France and taken his place at the head of Washington's cabinet. He came back with both body and brain dressed in the French fashion. His subtle, ingenious mind was full of the ideas of the French Revolution, then beginning in Paris. But except for his belief in liberty and humanity, which was born with him and which he did not go to Paris to learn, the wild ravings of the Jacobin clubs and the doctrines of Marat and Robespierre were as little a part of the real man as his French clothes. He would use the ideas of French democracy so long as they were useful and a fit covering for his real purposes, and then he would lay them aside as he did his French coat when it was worn out. With his mind thus occupied, Jefferson had come home to an America very different from the one he had left. A new government, with the inception and plan of which he had had but little sympathy, had been constructed, and the foundations of a

strong state were already rising among the ruins
of the old confederacy. He found a vigorous
party, led for the most part by new men, arrayed in defense of a strong central government,
and urging forward all measures calculated to
invigorate it. Opposed to them were a body of
men, numerous, it is true, but scattered and dis-
organized, with no possible party ground except
resistance to the Constitution and all its works.
Jefferson, with his keen perceptions, saw at a
glance the folly of opposition to the Constitution; but as he surveyed the field on which he
had just arrived it was by no means easy to
determine what position to take. Nevertheless,
while he waited and watched for developments,
he had to do something, and that something, as
was most natural, was to give his support to the
administration of which he was a part, and to
its measures, which then consisted of Hamilton's
financial policy, hanging in the balance on the
decision of Congress as to assumption. Jefferson saw as plainly as anybody the scope of the
financial policy and the intrinsic merit of assumption. He had, moreover, no prejudices at
that time against the author of the policy. With
no line marked out for his conduct, and ready,
until events decided otherwise, to sustain the
administration, he fell in easily enough with the
schemes of his colleague. There was a little talk

and a little dinner, and Hamilton agreed to secure votes for a southern capital, and Jefferson
promised to do the same for assumption. It
would be an error to treat this as a bargain or
compromise between opposing factions, for it
was the work of two cabinet ministers favoring
the same policy. Hamilton gained success for
his great plans. Jefferson by his personal influence helped to carry through the measures of
the administration of which he was a member,
and obtained in return the concession of the site
of the capital, which was of value to him as a
Southern leader. In after times, when Hamilton stood to Jefferson and his party as the
representative of all that was bad, the memory
of this transaction of 1790, and of a friendly
alliance with the great Federalist, became trou-
blesome. Jefferson would fain have erased from
history the whole business. He wished the world
to believe that the wicked, aristocratic, monar-
chical Federalists had always been his foes, and
had found in him their mightiest opponent. Yet
there was the ugly fact that he had himself
turned the scale in favor of one of their fundamental measures. His manner of dealing with
the problem was characteristic. He did not explain it away in his lifetime, for he might have
met with awkward contradiction. But he set it
all down for the benefit of posterity, and then

excused himself for having supported a measure
of the administration of which he was a member, and for having aided the accursed Federalists, by saying that he was "duped by Hamilton."

It is impossible to resist pausing over this
statement, for it is one of the most amusing ever
made even by Jefferson, and shows a confidence
in the credulity of posterity which is not flat-
tering. In justice to Jefferson it must be said
that, as long as he had made up his mind to get
himself out of what he considered a scrape, this
was the only excuse he could make. But it was,
unluckily, a most clumsy and transparent deception. Thomas Jefferson had his weaknesses and
his failings, but an imperfect knowledge of human nature and human character was not among
them. In the difficult art of understanding his
fellow men he was unrivaled, and he was never
deceived by any man, unless by himself and as
to his own motives. On the other hand, Hamilton was the very last man to succeed in duping
others, and it would be difficult to find anything
more impossible to Hamilton than the feat attributed to him by his rival. He had a directness of thought and action which was always
remarkable, and at times overbearing and intol-
erant. It may well be doubted whether he could
have successfully duped any one, even if he had

tried, and he certainly had far too much sense to have attempted such an experiment on so unpromising a subject as Jefferson.

But we are indebted to Jefferson, and to his inability to let well alone, for the details of this whole matter, since the other side held their tongues. The Federalists were not, as a party, given to useless chatter, while Hamilton as usual went straight to his mark, called out unexpected resources, and said nothing about it. Congress took up the funding measures again, and the old angry wrangling went on even after a disagreeable consciousness that they were beaten in some unknown way had crept over the opposition. When the decisive moment came, their fears were fully confirmed. The capital went to the Potomac and assumption was voted. The first great battle had now been fought in all its parts and the secretary had won.

The plans for the revenue, for the excise, for the mint, were adopted in principle, and substantially as Hamilton advised. The secretary's innocent suggestion, that the image and symbols on the coins might be made to have an educational bearing, led to a proposal to stamp on one side of the coins the head of the President for the time being. This harmless proposition produced a debate amusing to us, but very earnest, heated, and real a hundred years ago. The upshot of it all was the adoption of the head of Liberty for the coins, and the discussion has no value except as showing the state of public feeling. From this utterly insignificant controversy we see that when Hamilton sought to advance the cause of strong centralized government and of an aristocratic republic he was not crying in the wilderness. He appealed to clearly marked opinions, entertained by a body of men powerful by their talents if not by their numbers. On the other hand, there appears an immense amount of ill-defined sentiment cherished by a majority of the people, but in a party sense ill-regulated and incoherent, which turned longingly back toward the days of a shattered confederacy and sovereign States, which was thoroughly democratic, and looked with morbid suspicion on everything, no matter what, which tended to lend strength or dignity to the central government. It was this opposition which met Hamilton at every point, and which, as it felt his strong hand drawing the bonds of federal and national government more and more tightly, detected aristocracy in every public office, and scented monarchy in the image and superscription of the coins; while among the party of the secretary were to be found those who, with all their wise policy and high purposes, believed forms and titles essential not merely to dignity but to strength. The truth, as usual, lay somewhere between the extremes illustrated by the trifling symbols on which excessive partisans set a high price.

The next really great measure in the financial policy gave rise to a stubborn contest which was carried through both houses of Congress and into the cabinet, there to receive its final decision at the hands of Washington. The opposition, which had been aroused by the assumption of the state debts, to the strengthening and concentrating effect of the financial policy, cried out loudly against the additional bond of union disclosed in the bank. They railed against the class which was thus being bound to the government, and against the capitalists who were being brought to the side of the administration. They pointed out that the South and agriculture were sacrificed to the North and trade. But all was vain. Hamilton was now on the flood-tide of success, and the national bank passed by a good majority. The most formidable weapon employed against it was the constitutional argument used by Madison, and, as the President was known to have doubts on this point, the last and strongest stand was made in the cabinet. Jefferson, Randolph, and Madison severally gave Washington

written arguments against the bank. In great
haste and pressed by business, Hamilton made
the famous reply which has already been discussed, and which gained Washington's adherence. In defending the bank, Hamilton established the doctrine of the implied powers, — a
matter infinitely more potent and more far-
reaching than the establishment of the great
financial machine which called it forth.

The last of the reports, that on manufactures,
was economically more important than any of its
predecessors, but it had no immediate results.
Congress had already discussed the question
vaguely, and had done something to favor home
production and American commerce. The question of protection or free trade was constantly in
men's minds, but a system was of slow growth.
Hamilton pointed to the road to be followed,
and other men traveled in it, among the first
Jefferson and Madison with their plan of "allowances" for the fisheries, while at the same
time they denounced the theory, its author, and
all his works, including "protection and bounties." Hamilton marked out clearly and fully
a plan for the development of industry, trade,
and commerce. He turned the current of
thought, he influenced the future, but the task
was too mighty, the scheme was too vast to be
carried out at once, or in fact otherwise than

piecemeal, although its suggestion was a fit termination to the great work which he had accomplished.

Thus was the financial policy completed, adopted, and put in operation as Hamilton designed it. The only mischance was the speculation which began with the debt certificates, was fostered by the success of the bank, and expanded into a wild mania, and consequent panic and disaster. From the outset the secretary had striven to check this spirit, of which he saw the evil and danger. He repelled his friends who sought information, and did all that was possible to cool the excitement. He strove in vain, and then was blamed for the speculation, the rapid fortunes, and the swift disaster alike.

The only miscalculation made by Hamilton was in regard to the rate of interest, which he supposed would fall, but which, owing to the marvelous rapidity of material development and the consequent employment of capital, really rose. The error was almost unavoidable, and it was quite harmless. The criticisms which have been made on this famous series of measures have been various and contradictory. It was said at the time that Hamilton made the debt too permanent, but on the other hand it was also urged that he was putting too great a burden on the people, and the shorter the loan

the greater the immediate burden. In this he
observed a just mean and a wise moderation.
The unexpected rate of growth in the country
showed afterwards that the debt might have
been paid more rapidly, but at the moment
Hamilton's anticipations of revenue were generally regarded as absurdly sanguine. The most
forcible criticism, which was made either then
or since, was that the financial policy was too
strong, that it put too great a strain upon the
infant experiment, ventured too much, ran too
great a risk, and came near causing shipwreck.
Hamilton reasoned that, if his financial policy
could be made successful, a good national government might be built up, and that if it proved
too strong and the new system gave way, then
the Constitution was not worth preserving. Of
the soundness of this argument, as it seems to
me, there can be no doubt. But after all, the
best evidence is in results. There was no public
credit. Hamilton created it. There was no circulating medium, no financial machinery; he
supplied them. Business was languishing, and
business revived under the treasury measures.
There was no government, no system with life
in it, only a paper constitution. Hamilton exercised the powers granted by the Constitution,
pointed out those which lay hidden in its dry
clauses, and gave vitality to the lifeless instru-

ment. He drew out the resources of the country, he exercised the powers of the Constitution, he gave courage to the people, he laid the foundations of national government, — and this was the meaning and result of the financial policy.

CHAPTER VII

In carrying through his measures, Hamilton had found in the friends of the Constitution material for a political party. The Federalists, when the new scheme adopted by their efforts went into operation in March, 1789, were a very different body from that which stood about the administration after the passage of the treasury measures. When the first Congress assembled, the Federalists had achieved their immediate object, and were waiting for the progress of events. They were like a body of volunteers, who had rushed together to fight a battle immediately before them, and when the victory had been won and the enemy scattered they were but loosely held together, and, as they stood looking about rather vaguely, dispersion was quite as probable as organization. To the Federalists Hamilton came as a leader. He gave them new objects, he raised still higher the standard of better government, showed them how the Constitution was to be made to bear fruit, and that its adoption was merely the beginning of the great work for which they had come forward. When the financial policy was finally embodied in legislation, the band of volunteers had become a compact, well-disciplined army, a strong party with a policy which showed great things done, and stretched forward to the future, pointing out what was still to be accomplished. This was the political success of the financial policy, but it was not without its penalty to the triumphant Federalists in general and to Hamilton in particular.

If the Federalists in 1789 resembled a hastily gathered army of volunteers, their opponents were mere scattered bands of guerillas. Broken by the successful adoption of the Constitution, they wandered helplessly about, and gave way, with a good deal of spasmodic struggling, before the compact forces and sharp assaults of the Federalists. Their only bond of union had been resistance to the Constitution, and this not only became constantly weaker, but injured them by its very existence, as the popularity of the new system rapidly increased. Strong as they were in numbers, the Democratic party of the future had no better name than anti-Federalists, and no better cry than that of opposition to everything emanating from the government. This loose, incoherent mass was welded together by Hamilton's aggressive, decisive policy. It was

not much to do, but it at least compacted them,
so that if the Federalists presented, when the
National Bank Act passed, an appearance of
which any leader might be proud, they were
confronted by much more formidable opponents
than when they carried with a sweep the funding
of the domestic debt. The anti-Federalists had
not only consolidated themselves, but they had
concentrated their opposition with extraordinary
intensity upon one man. In those early days
Hamilton was thought by his opponents to be
the embodiment of all power, and as his policy
was developed before them he came to be considered the embodiment of all evil as well. His
followers at first seemed to have been regarded
largely as his creatures, and the dislike of the
anti-Federalists extended only very gradually
beyond the confines of the Treasury Department. The secretary was once more accused of
being " British " in his tastes and sympathies.
From England, his enemies declared, he had
borrowed everything. Nothing, it was said, was
original in the most successful financiering of
the time, and he was, according to his opponents,
preparing to go even farther, and was making
ready to introduce monarchy, aristocracy, and
the rest. Then came those hostile tributes to
his genius and ability which have never been
surpassed by the eulogies of his friends. To

Hamilton were attributed the sudden prosperity
and the wild speculation, while he was also held
responsible for not stopping the inevitable panic
to which speculation gave birth. Every member of the Federalist party was said to be personally inspired by the secretary, and to be
under the spell of his magical eloquence and
subtle reasoning; he had, as was alleged, bewitched and blinded the unerring judgment of
Washington, which had set the seal of its approval on the treasury policy. In attacks like
these, of little real weight, but nevertheless calculated as they increased in vehemence and repe-
tition to arouse enmity and impair his influence,
and in the drawing together of the opposition,
Hamilton found the dark side of his brilliant
success as a financier, a statesman, and party
leader. Still the attacks were as yet mere mut-
terings of a possible storm, for the anti-Federalists were after all very weak, with but little
ability except what Madison had brought over
to them, and were living a precarious life of
opposition solely for opposition's sake. They
needed a policy, direction and point in their
attacks; above all things they needed a leader.
They found all three at the right hand of Washington, in Hamilton's own colleague and quondam ally, Thomas Jefferson. The secretary of
state had made up his mind. He could no

longer support the administration. He could
not govern Hamilton, nor would he be ruled by
him, and his own State was wholly against the
government.   In Hamilton's successful policy
there were the germs of an aristocratic republic,
there were certainly limitations and possibly
dangers to pure democracy; he could not hope
to lead or control the Federalists, and therefore
nothing remained but to go to the leaderless
multitude on the other side and overthrow the
party of Washington and his great secretary.
This, it is needless to say, was not done in a
moment.   Jefferson was the last man to make
up his mind suddenly to a decisive step and
then take it at once.   He had no notion of cut-
ting adrift until he saw how the land lay.   Still
less ready was he to come boldly forward with
a programme and put himself at the head of a
party.   When he had his party all prepared he
would do this, but meanwhile he would stay
where he was.

It is impossible to fix the exact time when
the dissensions in the cabinet, where the new
party warfare took its rise, first definitely began.
When the flame leaped up before the eyes of
men, it was evident that the fire had been burning for some time.   We may say, however, in a
general way, that the "rift within the lute" began after the assumption of the state debts, and

was greatly widened by the differences among
the President's advisers as to the national bank.
It was in the winter of 1791–92 that Hamilton
became satisfied that Jefferson and Madison
were organizing and leading a party against
him; but at that time, and for some months to
come, he held his peace, and it would have been
well if he had continued to do so. The secret
work of Jefferson, who began his hostilities
against the administration before any one suspected him, and who continued them while
clinging to office long after his enmity toward
all his associates was notorious, first showed
itself in changes in the policy of the opposition.
In the first place, they got a name and called
themselves Republicans, as distinguished from
monarchists, the equivalent of Federalists. The
objects of opposition became better defined, and
were formulated in such a way as to be taking
cries and catchwords. A clear line of attack
was marked out, and in short, from being a confused crowd, the anti-Federalists began to assume the form and substance of a compact party.
This was the work of Jefferson, silent, subtle,
retiring, making no speeches, and printing no
essays, but doing a good deal of quiet talking
and shrewd letter-writing, toiling in the dark
and managing men. In the face of Hamilton's
dazzling success, to form an opposition party of

respectable character and good discipline, even
with abundant rough material at hand, was a
great political feat.   Even to make a beginning
took time, and the few points just mentioned
were the gradual developments of a twelvemonth.

Oddly enough, Jefferson's first blow — which
shows him turning to the opposition six months
before Hamilton suspected it — was hasty, and
unlike himself, because it was publicly given,
and fell not upon Hamilton but upon John
Adams.   That eminent man, finding but little
occupation for his restless energy in the vice-
presidency, betook himself to writing certain
essays entitled " Discourses on Davila."   These
articles, speculative in character, but well reasoned, and calculated to check the fervor excited
by the French Revolution, were very sound and
conservative in tone, advocated constitutional
government, checks and balances, upper houses,
and the like.   To Jefferson, entering upon the
path of a democratic leader, all this smacked of
monarchy and aristocracy, and he forthwith got
out an edition of Paine's " Rights of Man " as
an antidote to all such pernicious stuff, and pre-
fixed to it a preface in which he hit a sidelong
blow at the stout old patriot of Massachusetts.
John Quincy Adams replied as " Publicola."
Jefferson got the worst of this controversy,

and after his fashion tried to explain it all away. This affair, however, set him to reflecting on the fact, that while the Federalists had in "Fenno's Gazette" an organ devoted to their service, and reaching into every State, the party of the future had nothing of the sort. In the following autumn these meditations bore fruit in the shape of the "National Gazette," edited by Philip Freneau, to whom Jefferson gave the position of translating clerk in the State Department. Thus fortified, Freneau, who was a clever man and a versifier of some little talent, began a succession of bitter, sometimes of sharp and well-directed attacks upon the measures of the administration, and particularly upon Hamilton. Then it was that Hamilton, putting two and two together, came to the very accurate conclusion that Jefferson and Madison were organizing a party against him, and had established a newspaper in their interest as a very necessary part of the plan.

Jefferson, meantime, was at work in other directions. He wrote to Washington more than once, deprecating the treasury measures, and depicting a state of popular discontent, and stirred up others to do the same. At last, on a visit to Virginia during the summer of 1791, Washington heard from the lips of his "quondam friend," Colonel Mason, a long and adverse criticism upon the policy of the administration. Taking this as an excuse, perhaps Washington condensed all that had been written or said into a brief summary and sent it to Hamilton. Here we find the principles, or more properly the war-cries, of the opposition formulated for the first time with some clearness, and in every line we detect the cunning hand of the secretary of state. Reduced to its simplest terms, this piece of criticism amounts to this: that Hamilton was politically a very bad and dangerous man, who had heaped up a vast debt, which was a sore burden to the people, but which he would not let them pay immediately, notwithstanding their overtaxed condition, but which he had contrived to render permanent; that he fostered speculation, juggled with paper money and the debt in order to influence Congress, where he maintained a corrupt squadron; and that he was laboring secretly to introduce aristocracy and monarchy. Hamilton dealt with this diatribe in a way very characteristic of him when he kept his temper, as he usually did. After a few lines of quiet indignation in his reply to the President, he proceeded to number all the objections made by Mason, and then discussed and answered each of them in his usual cold, forcible, and lucid fashion, just as if he were drawing a report or making a brief, instead of repelling gross personal attacks. The task was not difficult, for where the accusations were not contradictory they were hopelessly and plainly false, and Washington was entirely satisfied. Indeed, it must be confessed that Jefferson's first declaration of party principles was a pretty poor one. But it was better than anything the party by itself had been able to do : it gave them some valuable catchwords, and concentrated their efforts on the ruin of one man.

Whether this last assault was too much for his endurance, or whether the " National Gazette," now ,more vituperative than ever, had become unbearable, it is certain that, after replying to the " Objections " sent him by Washington, Hamilton completely lost his temper. He descended into the arena of party strife, and proceeded to answer Freneau, and whip Jefferson over the shoulders of his editor. This was improper and undignified, — the act of an angry man, righteously indignant, no doubt, but not on that account to be excused for taking his high office into the dust of a political newspaper brawl. There was, moreover, no need of it. Federalist politicians and Federalist editors were never either slow or feeble with pen or tongue, and were quite capable of defending their chief and their party. But Hamilton had lost his temper, and a ready pen is a

terrible temptation. Once engaged, he fought
well, of course, and it may be admitted that he
gained a temporary advantage. It is no excuse
to say that all the leading men of the day wrote
for the newspapers, and formed public opinion
in that way. Hamilton was a member of the
cabinet, next to Washington the most conspicuous man in the country, and he had no right
and no business to send anonymous communications to the newspapers, savagely attacking
one of his colleagues in the administration. He
hurt his assailants badly, no doubt; he wrote
brilliantly; he gained a temporary victory, but
in the eyes of posterity he injured himself and
his personal and official dignity. Jefferson, we
may be sure, had not planned to draw Hamilton out. He never cared for debate either in
the newspapers or by word of mouth. He had
no love for a stricken field, and had doubtless
believed that circumstances would keep Hamilton silent. He winced terribly when Hamilton
rushed at him and publicly denounced him as
the supporter of a journal devoted to attacks on
the government, whose editor he provided for
by public office. He smarted under the lash of
a practiced hand, which depicted him as a secret
intriguer against the treasury measures, which
demolished his charges and laid bare all the
operations of the financial policy, with great

consequent credit to its author. For the time
being the " National Gazette " was crippled and
the secretary of state humiliated; but for this
poor reward Hamilton had deeply grieved and
troubled the President, who had watched the
well-directed shafts go home, and who keenly
felt the injury to the government and to the
country of such a quarrel, so conducted, and
between men occupying such positions. Washington remonstrated with both by letter, and
the replies bring the two secretaries into strong
contrast. Hamilton's letter was brief, direct,
and manly. He said little about his antagonist,
avowed his right to defend himself, and promised to do all in his power to keep the peace
and hold the administration together. Jefferson's answer was long and tortuous. He defended himself elaborately against Hamilton's
published attacks with a kind of wail in his
tone which showed that he had been hurt; but
he devoted most of his reply to Washington's
request for harmony to venomous and bitter
abuse of his colleague. As a practical result
of all this, Hamilton stopped his attacks, while
Jefferson opened fresh trenches in a new direction.

When Congress came together, Hamilton introduced a series of measures looking to the
speedy redemption of the debt. One was to

insure the maintenance of the sinking fund, and
provide for outstanding certificates; another,
to borrow money at a lower rate of interest;
and a third, to levy taxes to buy up the six per
cents as rapidly as possible. By the strenuous efforts of the opposition, the last two were
defeated; the proposition for new taxes, some
of which fell upon the planters who were accustomed to raise revenue in the North, being
particularly distasteful. Thus it was that the
party which denounced the debt, and accused
Hamilton of using it corruptly, met his proposal to take all possible reasonable steps for
its redemption, and, having done themselves all
they could to render it permanent, they yet
continued to assail the secretary for that very
design.

But all this was the mere disingenuousness
of party warfare. The next assault planned by
Jefferson and Madison was a much more serious affair. It aimed at the personal ruin of the
secretary, and was intended to drive him from
the cabinet and prove him guilty of corruption. The attack was headed by Giles, a rough,
brazen, loud-voiced Virginian, fit for any bad
work, no matter how desperate. First, accounts
of one foreign loan were called for, then of all;
then, when it appeared that two loans had been
consolidated for which there was but doubtful

authority in law, and while Jefferson was in-
sinuating to Washington that Hamilton had
used these loans corruptly to aid the bank,
there came a string of resolutions calculated
to lay bare every operation of the treasury.
Jefferson and Madison in this business made
the great mistake of not knowing their man before they fell upon him. They probably had
little real doubt of Hamilton's integrity, but
they thought he would find it difficult to de-
monstrate it by figures, — they thought that
in all these complicated finances there might
be errors susceptible of distortion which would
cause them to be misconstrued, and, above all,
they hoped that Hamilton would be so harassed
that he would leave the cabinet. They reckoned without their host. Hamilton was not
only a man of spotless integrity in his vast
financial transactions, but he was essentially a
fighting man. When danger of this sort came
upon him, his head became clearer and his nerve
greater than before. He was no longer the
party leader writing anonymously in " Fenno's
Gazette : " he was the great minister, called
upon without warning to defend himself, his
honor, his office, and his department. Now his
genius for organization told in the readiness with
which, under his system, everything could be
accounted for. Report after report poured in

upon Congress until every operation of the treasury was displayed to the public eye so plainly
that he who ran might read. Those who had
undertaken this ill-starred business would fain
have adjourned and left it all unsettled. But
Hamilton was too quick for them, and before
the session closed everything had been exposed
to the public gaze. The Federalists rejoiced, and
eagerly pressed their advantage. Giles introduced resolutions of censure, and the Federalists
forced a vote on all of them. Poor Madison,
who was preëminently a man of peace, but who
had been dragged into this as he was into all
his great mistakes by others, had no escape.
He was compelled to go on record in favor of
the resolutions in a minority so small that it
was at once ludicrous and humiliating when
contrasted with the grandeur of the preparation and the violence of the abusive declamation
which had accompanied the whole proceeding.

We know that the efforts made by Hamilton to accomplish this feat told severely on his
health, and the event is one of the most important in his career, because it brought out so
strongly the salient features of his mind and
character. Hamilton could organize and discipline bodies of men both in war and politics,
but he was not a party manager. He could
marshal his forces in debate as he marshaled

his arguments; he could lay out a policy and give directions to his lieutenants, but he could not deal with the rank and file. With his party behind him, he could lead; but others must manage the forces. With the same overwhelming impetuosity with which he charged the Yorktown redoubt, he now rushed upon Giles and upon those who moved the wires which made Giles dance. In the dash of the onset we see the vehement energy and strong passionate nature of Hamilton toiling day and night, until the color left his cheeks, that he might compel an issue before Congress adjourned. Yet in all this hot enthusiasm and defiance comes out the clear, cold, penetrating intellect which without an angry word could draw out schedules and balances and accounts, a long array of silent and convincing figures, and nothing else. When at last the conflict was over, and he had routed his opponents and stood flushed with victory, it is no wonder that the party chiefs gathered round him with a zealous devotion. The people saw that Hamilton had triumphed; that he had been right and his enemies wrong; that he had been clean and above reproach. But these long columns of figures did not appeal to the popular imagination, and the masses did not appreciate the magnitude of the battle which had been waged. The leaders in Congress and elsewhere

saw all this, and it was with them that Hamilton stood highest then and always.　There
was probably no one, however, who appreciated
the situation so keenly as Jefferson.　The most
desperate assault possible had been disastrously
repulsed.　Hamilton was higher than ever in
the public esteem, stronger than ever in the
estimation of his party, now rendered more aggressive and active than before.　He could not
be driven from the cabinet.　Direct attacks
upon him had clearly failed, and Jefferson made
no effort to take up the shivered lance, which he
had placed in another hand to use in the open
lists.　It only remained to stay in the cabinet
and there contend with Hamilton for supremacy
in guiding the course of the government and
winning the confidence and trust of Washington.

CHAPTER VIII

FOREIGN RELATIONS AND THE MAINTENANCE OF THE AUTHORITY OF THE GOVERNMENT

I DO not propose to deal here with the question of the foreign relations of the United States at this period, for the subject is one of the broadest scope, and fit only for a general history in the most comprehensive sense of the term. It was at this time that the foundation of the so-called Monroe doctrine was laid by Washington's proclamation of neutrality, which marked out the true foreign policy of the United States by declaring that this republic of the New World would hold itself aloof from the struggles of Europe. The policy thus laid down was one of the great corner-stones placed by the wisdom of Washington's administration, and upon which the fabric of national greatness was founded. To convert the doctrine of the neutrality proclamation into a guiding and fundamental principle of the state was the work of more than a quarter of a century, and upon our foreign relations during that period the history of the country turned. When they first come into prominence during Washington's first term, they mark the beginning of an important phase of our development. Between the proclamation of neutrality and the close of the war of 1812, this country adjusted its position among the nations of the earth, settled its foreign relations which then drew the political lines in the United States, and on which the fate of our parties hung, and completed the work of the Revolution by breaking the fetters of political thought as the war had severed the political bonds. In a word, for many years after the neutrality proclamation, the country was engaged in changing its ideas from those of colonies to those of a nation, and in struggling to make itself as independent mentally as it was politically. Into this broad and inviting field it is no part of my purpose to enter. My object is merely to show the place in it which Hamilton occupied, his opinions as to our foreign relations, and the part he took in shaping our foreign policy. Above all, I wish to depict his attitude in regard to the French Revolution, which convulsed the minds of men throughout the civilized world far beyond its own borders, far beyond the regions even where its armies penetrated, and of which it may be truthfully said that Hamilton was one of the most illustrious victims both in his life and in his death.

In March, 1789, our situation in regard to
foreign nations was anything but enviable.
England, with ill - concealed hatred, held the
Western posts, and refused, on account of the
unpaid debts of British subjects, to indemnify
us for the slaves which had been carried off
during the war. She flouted our ministers, refused to send a representative to this country,
and strove in every possible way to injure our
commerce, of which she had so lately enjoyed
a monopoly. Our relations with the mother
country were, in short, as strained and mutually
offensive as possible. With France, toward
whom we felt as a people a sincere gratitude,
they were hardly more favorable. Jefferson had
failed to obtain from that country any better
commercial treatment than was accorded by
England. With Spain there was a chronic quarrel, and a dark cloud of war and aggression
hung over the valley of the Mississippi. Hamilton felt that the first steps toward placing the
United States in the position which they ought
to occupy were the restoration of their credit and
reputation, and the display of order, strength,
and resources which this involved. He rightly
believed that success and stability would do
more than anything else to compel the respect
and consideration of the rest of the world. So
far as the various nations were concerned, while

as an individual citizen he was inclined by his
feelings toward France, as a statesman he clearly
saw that all nations must be treated alike; that,
owing to her geographical situation, America
had no such things as natural alliances and
enmities, but that at the same time on commercial grounds friendly relations with England
were vastly more important than with any other
nation of the earth. With England, too, the
objects at which Hamilton aimed would count
for more than anything else. Whatever incon-
sistencies England may have been guilty of, she
has never swerved in civility and respect for
success, strength, and wealth, and this Hamilton
well knew. But he did not reckon on this alone.
In his report on manufactures a cardinal principle was that of retaliation, and the hand he
meant thus to force was the hand of England.
At the same time he regarded the efforts to discriminate between the various nations, that is,
in favor of France and against England, on the
ground of gratitude to the one and hatred to
the other, as wholly false in principle. Such a
course would surely lead to further disagree-
ments with the latter; and the object of the
United States was not to indulge in sentiment,
but to build up its national greatness and grow
rich by its commerce. To treat all nations as
they treated us, and to bury the past, which

should not be allowed to hamper the new government, was Hamilton's theory. He had no attachment to England, but rather the contrary. He admired the British constitution as the best system of free government in existence; like all his fellow citizens, he had been nurtured amid the English traditions of law and government, and he had no question that English principles in respect to law and government were, with proper modifications, best suited to the United States. Toward France he felt both affection and gratitude, and in that country were many tried and loved friends and companions in arms. But he wished the new republic to lay aside all sentiment and prejudice as well as all inconvenient memories, and to start fair and free with a view only to her own interests, and a general determination to treat all nations alike if they all behaved equally well; to have no alliances, no friendships, and no enmities, but to cut loose from all complications and aim only at success.

Hamilton's theory as exemplified in the financial policy worked well. Evidences of respect abroad began to multiply. Washington, through Gouverneur Morris, sounded England in regard to the renewal of diplomatic relations, which had been practically severed since the day when John Adams had been driven away from St. James by a stupid insolence which England

has always been fond of displaying toward this
country, and which has cost her, first and last,
many bitter lessons. The result of Washington's experiment, backed by the rapidly growing prosperity of the country and the increasing
stability of the government, was the appointment of a minister to the United States in the
person of Mr. George Hammond. This gentleman was empowered to begin negotiations for a
commercial treaty, but could conclude nothing.
The reëstablishment of commercial relations on
a basis something like reciprocity was still distant enough, but nevertheless a good deal had
been gained by the mere renewal of diplomatic
intercourse. Hammond's negotiations were not
very fruitful, but they went on pretty steadily,
and Hamilton took a considerable share in them
from time to time, more, it must be confessed,
than strictly belonged to him as secretary of the
treasury. The truth was that Hamilton had a
policy for the new government in every direction as well defined as in financial affairs, and
he strove to put each and all into effect. He
could not rid himself of the idea that he was
really the prime minister, a notion encouraged
by the way in which Congress had thrown all
sorts of questions into his hands for decision.
Moreover, his schemes deserved and won the
confidence of Washington; and the result was

that Jefferson, entirely innocent of clear-cut, sharply defined plans and policies, and waiting to be guided by events, found himself, much oftener than was pleasant, pushed aside, ridden over, and, as in the case of Hammond, more or less interfered with.

While the United States were thus making their way into the family of nations the French Revolution began, and in a few years the newly launched ship of the young republic was tossing on the waves of the terrible storm which found its centre in Paris. The first news of the great movement in France was received in this country with universal pleasure and delight by men of all shades of political belief. As to the benefits of a free constitution in a country toward which we felt so warmly, all persons—the ultra-Federalist and the radical opponent of the administration alike — were agreed and had a common gratification. But the rapid changes rolled on, and one event succeeded another, each with terrible logic more dreadful than the last, and all hurrying to the worst extremes of violence. When reform became revolution, revolution anarchy, and redress revenge, — when hot-blooded killings in the street changed to cold-blooded massacre and cowardly murder in the prison and the palace, culminating at last in the execution of the king and the daily slaugh-

ter of the guillotine, — then public opinion in
America shifted. First the timid and suspicious
began to doubt, then the more cautious began to
fear, then such men as Washington and Hamilton lost sympathy with a battle for freedom
fought in this wise, and the latter rebelled
against comparing the French Revolution with
our own, saying, "The one is liberty, the other
licentiousness." The general enthusiasm with
which the French Revolution had been greeted
faded away; but while that conflict became distasteful to the mass of the people and an object of suspicion and dislike to the Federalists,
the revolutionary fever strongly infected certain
elements which predominated among the enemies of the administration. As one side headed
by Washington and Hamilton cooled towards
France, the other side grew proportionately hot-
ter in admiration and love for the principles of
the revolution, just then becoming rather wild
and uncertain. This widening rift between two
bodies of public opinion was certain before long
to breed a party issue. So long as men watched
events in Paris and came to one conclusion or
another as a matter of abstract theory, no harm
was done, but sooner or later these conclusions
would be brought to the touchstone of practical
decision, and then the parties which had been
evoked by the revolution would begin a fierce

conflict.   Early in April, 1793, the news arrived
that war had been declared between England
and France, and that a new minister from the
terrible republic had reached Charleston.   The
decisive moment had come, and Hamilton sent
post-haste for Washington, who was at Mount
Vernon.   When the President reached Philadelphia, he found his two secretaries prepared
to meet the crisis, the gravity of which no member of the administration doubted, but prepared
to meet it in ways very different and highly
characteristic of the two men.   Jefferson loved
France and the ideas of the revolution, and he
hated England; but he also dreaded war and
had no desire to have the United States drawn
into hostilities.   Under these circumstances he
was unable to make up his mind as to any definite plan.   In order therefore to get, if possible, an expression of public opinion and thereby
come to a determination and be rid of responsibility, he proposed to call Congress at once in
extra session.   It is probable that he saw an
opportunity to make party capital by the agitation of this subject in debate, but a summons to
Congress was at all events the only suggestion
he had to offer to Washington.

Hamilton on the other hand cared for neither
England nor France, except so far as he loathed
the bloody anarchy of the one and respected the

stability and order of the other. His thoughts
were fixed on the United States, unbiased by a
sentiment for or against any other nation. For
the United States he dreaded war almost as
much as Jefferson, but unlike his colleague he
had not the slightest doubt as to the position
to be taken at that trying moment, and he had
fully made up his mind as to the true policy to
be adopted. Hamilton had no desire to shift
the responsibility of a duty which he conceived
to belong to the executive, and which he also
thought would be far safer in the hands of
Washington than if it were tossed about in a
legislative body. He had no wish, therefore, to
have Congress called together; but he prepared
a series of questions embodying his views, and
these he submitted to Washington, who laid
them before the cabinet. The policy outlined
by these questions was the maintenance of a
strong, strict, and genuine neutrality by the
United States, to which the utmost publicity
should be given, and then a careful consideration of our relations with France, in order that
the past might not be so construed as to entangle us with the fortunes and conflicts of the
revolution, and in that way drag us from our
true position of absolute neutrality and consequent peace. The first question, as to issuing
a declaration of neutrality, was carried in the

affirmative, and the proclamation to that effect soon appeared. This was really the central point of the whole policy of Washington and Hamilton, and was one of the great landmarks established by the Federalists for the guidance of the republic. There is no stronger example of the influence of the Federalists under the lead of Washington upon the history of the country than this famous proclamation, and in no one respect did the personality of Hamilton impress itself more directly on the future of the United States. So little was it understood at the time that when thirty years later the same principle, in an extended form, was enunciated by Mr. Monroe's administration, it was hailed as a new doctrine, and incorporated as a leading article in the political creed of the United States. When adopted and put forth by Washington, this truism of to-day was hardly appreciated. The colonial spirit, which was the spirit of the past, made it seem impossible that the United States should be wholly apart from the affairs of Europe. The Federalists acted on the principle thus laid down while they held power, maintaining a bold and strong neutrality, and ready to strike the first nation, no matter which it was, that dared infringe it. After the fall of the Federalists this doctrine slipped out of sight. For a vigorous neutrality, ever on the alert and ready for war, was substituted a timid, exasperating policy of peace protected by commercial warfare. Ten years of bitter political conflict, including three years of foreign war, was the result, and by this harsh process the colonial spirit was finally exorcised. Then the national foreign policy, formulated, devised, and adopted by Washington and Hamilton, was popularly accepted under the administration of Monroe.

The primary question of neutrality was settled by the proclamation. It then became necessary to fix the character of this neutrality by a careful determination of our attitude towards the most aggressive, active, and dangerous of the belligerents, — the French republic. The second point therefore came on the reception of the minister of France, which was settled in the affirmative. Then followed a series of perplexing questions as to receiving the minister with or without qualifications, and as to our relations to France under existing treaties. Up to this point the cabinet had succeeded in reaching an agreement, but now they diverged widely. Hamilton wished it distinctly understood that by receiving the French minister the United States did not admit that the treaties were now binding in their full extent. These treaties provided, of course, for the payment of our debt to

France, and also for the guarantee of the French possessions on this continent, and for a defensive alliance. Hamilton, who at the outset had done his best to expedite payments to the new government, had more recently begun to hold back. He now said that while there was no doubt of the general rule of international law, that for treaty purposes the existing government was to a foreign nation the same as any predecessor, yet this rule, like all others, required reasonable construction. The change of government in France, he added, was of such a nature as to alter every circumstance under which and for which the treaties had been made, and therefore the United States had the right to renounce them. Moreover, everything was so uncertain and shifting in France that to live up to the treaties with the present government might in a few months amount to a cause of war with its successor. Again, the war was not defensive, and so Hamilton concluded that all this should be plainly stated to the minister, so that he might understand that we did not intend to be bound by the treaties. Hamilton's construction was, at least, that of the French Convention, which had just annulled a clause in one of the treaties, but it was also the sound and statesmanlike view. His arguments go to great length, and are clear and acute, as usual, but the central

idea was as simple as it was wise. The French
treaties were legacies of the past. They were
colonial in spirit and in fact. The opportunity
had now come to be rid of them legally and
fairly. Hamilton's entire policy was to take immediate advantage of the opportunity, cut loose
from these entangling bonds, and thus assume
in foreign affairs a wholly free and thoroughly
national position. Jefferson, on the other hand,
was for a rigid construction of the law of nations
and for the maintenance of the same close connection with the republic as with the monarchy,
always barring actual war.

These contending views, however, and a decision upon them, were soon pushed aside by
the appearance in person of Genet, the minister
himself, who raised a series of difficult and exasperating questions of the most practical kind so
quickly that there was no time to consider general policies. The administration found enough
to do in checking Genet's mischief without
coming to any conclusion as to the qualifications with which he should be received, or as
to the statements which should be made to him
with reference to the attitude of the United
States in regard to the treaties. The policy
of the United States toward France was, indeed,
settled during these contests with her representative, and ultimately according to Hamilton's

doctrines, but it was done bit by bit, in sore
vexation of spirit, and not broadly, comprehen-
sively, and quietly.

Indeed, from the time when Genet came upon
the scene, a settlement in the latter fashion was
out of the question. The new minister was an
excitable, light - headed Frenchman, maddened
by the wild ideas of Paris. He rushed from
one excess to another from the day of his arrival until that on which his successor appeared,
and he endeavored to raise about him a party
to overthrow the administration. His first act
was to fit out privateers at Charleston, and
thence proceed with a sort of triumphal procession northward to Philadelphia. Difficulties
now gathered thickly about the cabinet. The
fitting out of privateers and the capture of prizes
by these privateers, as well as the seizure of
British vessels within our waters, all leading to
expostulation and demands for redress on the
part of the English minister, confronted the
administration in a constant succession of cases.
Hamilton, whose policy was not neutrality with
a covert leaning to one side, but a genuine neutrality treating all alike, took strong ground in
favor of at once giving up the prize made by
a French ship of war within our waters. He
also urged the immediate stoppage, by all the
force of the government, of the enlistment of sea-

men and fitting out of privateers by the French
in our ports, and the surrender of all prizes of
such privateers, or, if restoration was impossible, then compensation on our part to the
owners wherever we had failed in our duty as
a neutral. The first point prevailed at once.
The third was resisted by Jefferson as too much
in favor of England, and as amounting to re-
prisal. For a time decision on this point was
suspended, but ultimately Hamilton's view received the sanction of Washington. On the
fitting out of privateers a long struggle ensued
between the French minister and the administration. Here a privateer would be stopped,
and there one would escape. Americans were
arrested and tried for infractions of neutrality
by enlisting on the French privateers; and at
last French consuls, who were undertaking to
govern in this country as their fellows did in
the states of Europe bordering on the terrible
republic, were deposed from office and deprived
of the right to exercise their functions. This
fitting out of privateers finally culminated in
the case of the Little Sarah, sent forth from
Philadelphia in flagrant contempt of the government, and beneath the very eyes of the cabinet. Hamilton and Knox urged strongly and
characteristically the duty of placing a battery
on one of the islands, and of firing upon the

privateer if she attempted to escape. Thanks to Jefferson, however, who believed, or pretended to believe, that Genet had promised not to let the vessel go, and who was in a tremor at the idea of joining in "the combination of kings" and getting into war with France, Hamilton's plan was not carried out, the militia were withdrawn, and Genet sent the privateer at once to sea. Washington came back in a state of indignation, and Jefferson found himself so thoroughly uncomfortable that he now seriously thought of resignation.

In other quarters Genet was equally active. He made a continuous effort to get all the money due to France. He anticipated payments so far as he could and then asked for more, and almost insisted that he should receive the whole amount either in money or provisions. But in the domain of the treasury Hamilton was master and unrestrained. Genet's loud demands passed idly by. The secretary paid him what was due, allowed him a reasonable anticipation, and could not be moved to do more. When the Frenchman threatened to give notes on the United States for what he wanted, in order to fit out privateers and illegal armaments in the Southwest against Spain, Hamilton gave him to understand that he might draw if he so pleased, but that his drafts would not be honored. It is refreshing, amid the bewildering complications of that confused time, to see the vain beating of the Frenchman at the doors of the treasury, and the perfect success of Hamilton's cool, unalterable attitude.

Genet, however, made even more trouble for the administration in our own politics than he did in the management of foreign relations. The sober and intelligent opinion of the country had turned away in disgust from the excesses of the French Revolution, but this opinion was silent and observant, and as yet inactive. On the other hand, the thoughtless and careless, the rabble in the larger cities, the foreign refugees from England and Ireland, and the more violent elements of the opposition were infected by the excitement of the French. In contemplating the objects of the movement in Europe, they overlooked the terrible means employed, and allowed their reason to be confused by the extravagant jargon of the new republic. The noise and enthusiasm were therefore with Genet. Banquets and processions, red caps and democratic societies, and the ravings of Freneau and Bache in their newspapers, all brought the half-crazed Frenchman to believe that the people were with him, and that through them he could force the government to do his pleasure. This agitation became so violent that Hamilton felt it to be necessary to evoke and give a lead to the opposite sentiment; and in the summer of 1793 he published a series of essays, signed "Pacificus," defending the proclamation and the policy of the administration. These papers, written in Hamilton's clear, convincing fashion, served their purpose of awakening the better part of the community to the gravity of the situation, and began the work of rallying the friends of the government to its active support. Calmly but steadily the administration persisted in carrying out its policy, despite every obstacle, foreign or domestic, and in the neutrality rules of August they laid down the principles of Washington and Hamilton as those by which they meant to stand, and by which the country should be guided in its foreign relations.

Genet's language and the tone of his letters increased continually in violence, and became at last so intolerable that the cabinet agreed to send his correspondence to Paris and ask for his recall. It was also resolved to furnish him with copies of this correspondence and of the demand for recall. Jefferson, whose private intercourse with Genet had been very different from his official attitude, warmly opposed this disclosure, fearing that it would lead to an outbreak. Hamilton, on the contrary, with all his fighting qualities now thoroughly aroused,

wanted to go much farther. He wished in the
first place that the recall should be made in
sharp and peremptory terms. He advocated,
also, the immediate publication of all the correspondence, and a direct appeal to the people. To this proposition Washington inclined,
but Jefferson succeeded in defeating it. Genet,
however, soon made the appeal himself, by pub-
lishing a letter which raised a direct issue between the President and himself. The tide of
public sentiment now turned strongly. The ruling elements in the community came forward,
the administration found itself supported, the
armaments in the West were checked, and the
French consuls brought to terms or deposed.
Again Hamilton and Washington wished to go
farther and suspend Genet from the exercise
of his functions, and again Jefferson checked
and prevented decisive action. The result was
that Genet went on for a few months longer in-
sulting our government, and doing a good work
in stimulating the public resentment against
France, but his power for mischief ended when
he appealed to the people against Washington.

Hamilton's course in all these complications
is highly characteristic. After carefully watching events in Europe, he advocated, when war
was declared, a sharply defined and strict neutrality, and then a firm but cautious severance

of all the entangling bonds which held us to
France. But when Genet appeared with insults
and aggressions, instead of negotiations and dis-
cussions, Hamilton, while still urging the rigid
enforcement of a genuine neutrality, wished to
lay aside diplomacy with the French minister,
and rebuke him openly and severely. He had,
moreover, no desire for the assistance of Congress, but preferred to have the Executive deal
with the whole matter and meet every compli-
cation as it arose. Jefferson acted simply as a
drag on the policy of his colleague, which, nevertheless, finally prevailed at every point; and it
is perhaps in some degree due to the opposition
of the secretary of state that the administration
came through all these trials so successfully.
Washington sympathized with Hamilton's views
and ultimately gave his approval to them all.
When Washington was angry, — as he was on
one or two occasions in this eventful summer, —
he was to the full as combative as Hamilton.
It is very conceivable that there were moments
when they might have moved too fast and struck
too hard, if it had not been for the persevering
resistance of Jefferson. But, however this may
have been, the policy of a strong and impartial
neutrality triumphed and was put in practice.
At every step the two secretaries went farther
apart, the one pushing on the successful policy,

the other holding back, clinging to the French
treaties, and professing that everything, neutrality and all, depended on the sanction of Congress.
The summoning of that body was another point
on which Jefferson had suffered defeat, and all
this, joined to the false position in which he was
placed, by holding one language officially, and
another privately to Genet, by taking one attitude with his party friends and another in the
cabinet, led to his resignation, which he with
reluctance deferred until the assembling of Congress.

When that body came together, the wisdom
of not calling it before was plainly manifest.
Genet had succeeded in one thing. He had
created a party issue, and had given a definite
object to the motley masses of the opposition.
The financial policy dropped out of sight, and
the now united opponents of the administration
fell with a swoop upon our foreign relations.
Everything conspired to help them. While our
government was trying to preserve neutrality
and keep the country out of the current of the
French Revolution, Great Britain had begun
that course of arrogant, aggressive interference
with our commerce which was perhaps the
stupidest blunder she made in her protracted
struggle with France, and which continued until
it produced war in 1812. This conduct gave

the opposition precisely the handle they wanted. Then, too, Jefferson was enabled, just before he left office, to map out the course to be pursued by sending in to Congress all his correspondence with Genet and Hammond, and a report on our commerce which indicated that policy of commercial warfare destined in later years to become such a curse to the country. Hamilton, who appreciated the party purposes to be gained by this, opposed the transmission of the Hammond correspondence; but Washington, who always rose above party, rightly decided that everything must go in.

In his dealings with Genet, Jefferson had been under the supervision of the cabinet, and his work was therefore spirited and strong, while with Hammond he needed no incentive to take a bold attitude. The correspondence therefore, as a whole, was vigorous in tone, and having all the ability for which Jefferson was conspicuous in letter-writing, deserves a high rank among our state papers. Invigorated by their leader's success, the opposition at once took up the line he had marked out in his commercial report, — which was by no means a very able document, — and Madison introduced resolutions to establish duties against nations not in treaty with us. Hamilton knew that the more eminent leaders on his side would meet this question in their

own way, but this did not content him. He
could not reply to Madison personally, but he
determined to do it through the mouth of another. He therefore equipped his friend, Mr.
Smith of South Carolina, with a speech, and
in this way met Madison at the outset of the
undertaking. Smith's reply, thus provided, was
strong and effective. The secretary lifted the
question at once out of the confusion of foreign politics, and placed it on purely commercial
grounds, arguing against the resolution on his
constant principles that in trade this country
should know neither friend nor enemy, but be
governed wholly by its interests. The argument was unanswerable, but the House passed
the resolution against which it was directed.
To the second resolution Nicholas offered an
amendment, naming England as the object of
the hostile discrimination; but his own party
was not ripe for this step, and the whole matter
was postponed. Then came a fresh and worse
aggression on the part of England in the form
of an order in council to seize all vessels loaded
with French produce. As ready to resent attack from one quarter as from another, Hamilton declared this order an outrage, and urged
the fortification of the seaports and the immediate raising of troops. The Federalists in the
House, adhering like their leaders to the doc-

trines laid down by Washington, sprang forward
with strong measures for an army, a navy, and
an embargo, in order to prepare the country for
war, which seemed indeed close at hand. The
opposition, always prodigal heretofore of brave
words, now held back, and stoutly resisted practical fighting measures, opposing particularly
the bill to establish a navy, which subsequently
became law. They were ready enough for party
purposes to declaim against England, to talk
war and yet keep the peace. They were quite
prepared to sequestrate debts, — a piece of swindling denounced by Hamilton, — and be as offensive as possible to England, but they were
not half so ready to fight with their kinsmen as
were the " British " Federalists. It was plain
that the country was drifting rapidly into war,
which Washington saw clearly would be most
perilous to the fortunes of the young nation.
Hamilton's idea of a special mission to England
met, therefore, with the warm approval of Washington, who at once turned to his secretary of
the treasury as the fittest man for this delicate and important task, an opinion in which he
was fully sustained by the Federalist leaders.
But the Virginia party, headed by Madison and
Monroe, greatly alarmed at the prospect of this
appointment, made an active and bitter resistance. Washington, anxious above all things for

the success of the mission, and in order to prevent the country from being torn with faction in
the face of these foreign troubles, gave up his
first choice and sent Jay, at the urgent recom-
mendation of Hamilton himself. The opposition in the Senate was bitter, but the nomination was confirmed; and Jay's instructions,
drawn in outline by Hamilton, were toned down
and then adopted by the cabinet. There are few
acts in our history which show greater force,
courage, and address than were displayed by
Washington and Hamilton in carrying through
this appointment despite every obstacle and the
most determined opposition which, even while it
acquiesced in the selection of the envoy, sought
by every means to hamper him and precipi-
tate war. Under the circumstances it must be
admitted that Washington was judicious. Yet
Hamilton would undoubtedly have made a better treaty, and one more satisfactory to the
country than that obtained by Jay. With all
the senseless clamor about his British sympathies, Hamilton would have aimed to get as
much as possible from England by taking a
high tone in the negotiation. This was shown
by his draft of instructions, which were modified
by the cabinet, in the direction of greater concessions to the English demands. He appreciated
as entirely as any one the necessity of peace,

and had plenty of tact and address, but he was far firmer, bolder, and more audacious than Jay, and these were the very qualities which were needed. The Jeffersonians were justly alarmed. If Hamilton made a successful treaty he would be stronger and more popular than ever, and it would all redound to the credit of his party and to his own dreaded influence. If, on the other hand, he should make a treaty which conceded much to England, he would probably force it through the Senate, and we should then be closer to England and farther than ever from France. With these views the outcry against Hamilton was started. It may well be doubted whether by the most virulent resistance the opposition could have done much harm, but it was possible that they might, and therefore Washington prudently decided as he did. At all events, the appointment of Jay, a more conciliatory policy on the part of England, and the appearance of Fauchet to take Genet's place, brought an interval of calm in our foreign difficulties, and permitted the administration to congratulate itself on the skill with which it had steered through the perils and complications of the past six months.

We have already seen the tendency of Hamilton in mind and temperament to distrust a pure democracy, and to have faith only in a

strong government and in the influence and
power of the upper classes, even if those classes
did not find, as he thought they should, direct
recognition in the Constitution.   This tendency
was turned into settled conviction as a matter
of general principle by the spectacle presented
to his observation in Paris.   When the matter,
however, was brought directly home to him by
Genet, by the popular support of France, and
by the wild talk of the opposition press and
speakers, Hamilton passed rapidly from the general to the particular, and began to believe not
only that pure democracy was abstractly perilous, but that there were in this country, as in
France, elements which considered democracy
and anarchy as convertible terms, and were bent
on producing the latter.

In what he called the "political putrefaction"
of Pennsylvania, and in the disturbances of the
western region of that State, Hamilton found,
as he thought, a practical manifestation of the
justice of his views as to the dangerous elements
in our population.   At last, too, the time had
come when a pacific policy towards the malcon-
tents was plainly impossible, and Hamilton was
allowed to deal with what he deemed the elements of anarchy as he thought they should be
dealt with, for it is unnecessary to say that Hamilton, for this contingency also, had a policy,

obvious and simple enough, it may be admitted, but still well-defined and thorough in details. The trouble had, in truth, been for some years coming to a head. The only serious criticism of Hamilton's financial policy is that it was too strong, that it strained the new fabric too severely, and this criticism always seeks proof in the excise law, which had been rendered necessary by the assumption of the state debts. Apart from the unanswerable economic arguments in favor of taxing spirits, Hamilton believed that unless the government could enact and enforce such a proper law the system of the Constitution was really worthless. The need of revenue carried the Excise Bill through Congress, in 1791, despite much bitter opposition. Its passage was the signal for the immediate display of a lawless and riotous temper in western Pennsylvania, where the manufacture of whiskey was chiefly carried on, and thence it spread rapidly through the similar regions of Virginia and North Carolina. At the next session, amendments perfected and modified the obnoxious law, while Hamilton devised every method to render its execution as easy as possible.

Still the disorders went on, until in the summer of 1792 they reached such a point that Hamilton, tired of the dilatory and ineffective

processes of law, thought the moment had come
for the direct and decisive application of force.
Washington, however, was not ready for extreme measures, and so Hamilton drafted a
proclamation, which Washington sent to Jefferson, who countersigned it, declaring privately
that he wholly disapproved it. The proclamation and Washington's journey through the
South had a good effect, and the disorder subsided in Virginia and North Carolina. But
in Pennsylvania the state of affairs continued
to grow steadily worse, and the opposition to
Hamilton's vigorous attempts to enforce the
law grew more violent. Finally, Congress gave
the executive additional powers, which were
sorely needed, but their exercise was the signal for armed resistance to the officers of the
United States. From gross and brutal out-
rages upon property and persons, the insurgents
passed to open defiance of the law. The United
States mail was stopped, large bodies of armed
men gathered, and the speeches and publica-
tions of the leaders proclaimed the overthrow
of the government. The emergency had come
and Washington met it, as he did every crisis,
calmly, firmly, and successfully. Hamilton was
at his side, ready with every detail. He had
carefully and characteristically estimated the
number of men capable of bearing arms in the

Insurgent counties, and knew precisely how many troops would be needed. The States responded to the call of the President, and with fifteen thousand men the administration faced the incipient rebellion.

Hamilton, after his own energetic fashion, wanted to serve as an officer, but finding this impracticable accompanied Washington and the army, and later went on without the President in general superintendence of the operations. It was his policy, and he was determined to carry it through even at the point of the bayonet, if the ordinary machinery of the law proved powerless. An attempt at negotiation was made by the frightened and more cautious among the leaders of the insurrection. The government readily gave them this last chance, but the conference came to nothing, and the army moved forward and spread through the disaffected region. Then the insurrection faded helplessly and bloodlessly away. It disappeared not only completely, but ridiculously and with humiliation to the vanquished. Gradually the disaffected came in and submitted, and were treated with the leniency which is so strong a trait in the American character. Hamilton himself showed a forbearance not a little remarkable in a man of his bold and imperious nature. But he was too wise to seek punish-

ment or revenge. He had triumphed. His
policy was vindicated. It had not been too
strong for the government, but had shown, on
the contrary, the force and vitality of the new
system. The power put forth had been simply overwhelming, and insurrection had been
crushed without leaving any memory of blood-
shed to rankle in the hearts of the people. The
financial policy had in truth converted the system of the Constitution into a living, vigorous
organism, and the unshrinking exercise of force
by the administration, which was wholly due to
Washington and Hamilton, brought to the government new strength, vigor, and respect. The
suppression of the " whiskey rebellion " had
shown the government to be capable of maintaining itself against armed resistance. The
lesson of Shays rebellion had not been wasted,
and the contrast thus afforded between the government of the confederacy and that of the Constitution was the crown of the masterly domestic
policy which had been begun by the first report
on the public credit.

When Congress came together the victory
of the administration was apparent in the en-
feebled action of the opposition, and the Federalists were not slow to take advantage of it.
Among Genet's legacies, and by far the most
objectionable, were the Democratic societies,

so called, modeled on the famous "clubs" of
Paris. They were worthless, noisy assemblages,
given to useless agitation. Hamilton, perhaps,
saw in them the same capabilities for mischief,
the same anarchical tendencies, as in their Parisian prototypes, but both he and Washington
and the Federalists generally considered them
dangerous, obnoxious, and by their clamorous
folly largely responsible for the outbreaks in
Pennsylvania. Washington, therefore, strongly
sustained by Hamilton, smote them with all
the force of his rarely used personal influence
and popularity. He denounced them in his
message ; the Senate supported him, and after
a heated debate in the House the opposition,
despite their majority, were unable to protect
their beloved associations. The blow, sharply
struck and well calculated in point of time, was
decisive. The societies withered away, and Genet's work was at an end. This closed the first
chapter in the history of the struggles growing
out of the French Revolution. The administration had come through this period of trial with
perfect success. Neutrality had been established and maintained, the wild sympathy with
France had been checked and discredited, domestic insurrection had been put down, and nationality had been advanced and strengthened
beyond all former expectations.

At the session of Congress in the previous year, when the opposition were throwing themselves upon our foreign relations, delighted to abandon the financial questions where they had suffered such defeat, Hamilton, with the fixed purpose that the attacks upon his character should not rest where they were, demanded further investigation. The most searching scrutiny was of no avail, and the opposition were more than ever disgusted with their mistake. After the lapse of another year Hamilton put the finishing touch to the funding system by a comprehensive scheme for the redemption of the entire debt. While this measure was on its passage, and after the galling results to the opposition of their investigation were well known, he laid down his office and retired from public life. He had been for some time contemplating this step, which had become imperative on account of his private affairs, and of the absolute need of an increased income to provide for his large family. He had been in office for nearly six years, and his work was done, his opinions and his personality were indelibly impressed upon our frame of government and upon our political development. We look in vain for a man who, in an equal space of time, has produced such direct and lasting effects upon our institutions and history.

CHAPTER IX

IF anything could have kept Hamilton in the
cabinet it would have been a knowledge of the
crisis which was to arise upon the reception of
the Jay treaty. He was, of course, well aware
of the fierce opposition excited by the creation of
the mission; he knew of the public meetings,
of the ravings of extreme Democrats, both in
the newspapers and on the platform, and of the
burnings in effigy of the excellent and eminent
ambassador. But he regarded all these things
as temporary ebullitions, which, as he foresaw,
died away into quiet while Jay was carrying on
his negotiations with Lord Grenville. Hamilton perceived, too, that, apart from the outward
manifestations, there was a profound interest in
the result of Jay's mission, and that there would
be a party conflict over its ratification. At
the same time he certainly did not anticipate
that such a shock would be produced as that
which actually occurred when the contents of
the treaty became known. But then Hamilton

did not expect such a result from the special mission. Rumor, speaking to us in the person of Jefferson, says that Hamilton called it an "old woman's treaty" when he first read it. To his penetrating mind and bold, dashing temperament, it may well have seemed that such an epithet was just. The treaty was certainly not such a one as he himself would have made. But he was called upon to deal with it as it stood, and on the broad ground of whether it should be accepted with all its defects, or rejected in favor of almost certain war.

The treaty went to the Senate, was ratified there, except the highly objectionable prohibitory clause in the twelfth article, and then went back to the President for final decision. Through the closed doors of the Senate the treaty slipped out, and was soon public property. When it became known, there was an outburst of popular indignation which has hardly ever been equaled in the history of the country. The wrath excited was partly justifiable, for some of the stipulations were far from what had been reasonably expected, and the fire was assiduously fanned by the partisans of France. The people judged hastily, and, in large measure, without reflection. The tempest swept through the country, accompanied with violent denunciation, insults to the British flag, rioting, burning in effigy, and every species of wild disorder; even the sturdy Federalist States of New England were swept from their moorings, and joined in the general outcry.

In the midst of all the hurly-burly stood Washington, calm, watchful, unterrified, making up his mind silently, and with "truth only for his guide." Here and there a few of the coolest and wisest among the Federalists saw the necessity of ratification and of standing by the President, and with their accustomed boldness and ability they faced the apparently hopeless odds arrayed against them. Foremost among them was Hamilton, ever present where the fray was thickest, and always first to come forward when a fight, especially if it was a desperate one, was in progress. He appeared at a great public meeting in New York to endeavor to check the raging opposition by fair discussion. Debate then and there was out of the question. Persuasive eloquence had for the moment lost its charm, and when Hamilton began to speak he was howled down and assailed with a volley of stones, one of which struck him on the forehead. With perfect coolness he said, "If you use such striking arguments, I must retire," and withdrew from a contest which at the moment was hopeless. But he retreated only to enter another field. Four

days after he had been stoned appeared the first
number of the series of essays signed " Camillus," in defense of the treaty, in favor of the
neutrality and peace policy, and in support of
the administration.

These essays continued to appear for a year,
and until the weight of public opinion was once
more on the side of their author. " Camillus "
was singularly effective, and the best proof of
his power came from his adversaries. Jefferson was particularly disturbed. He felt very
keenly the truth of Burr's remark, that any one
who put himself on paper with Hamilton was
lost. At the same time he was willing and
even anxious that some one else should run the
risk of wreck in a conflict with " the Colossus
of the Federalists," and he therefore urged the
unattractive duty upon Madison. That gentleman, however, had as little stomach for the
fight as his chief, and prudently held back.
Others less able and less wary than their leaders entered the field with replies of various
merit and various classical signatures, and were
beaten and driven off. Whatever may be said
of Hamilton in other respects, in political controversy, in the art of moulding, creating, and
controlling public opinion by discussion and
debate in the newspapers, he stood absolutely
without a rival. Ready, persuasive, transparent

in reasoning, and formidable in retort, he never
failed, when he took up his pen, to create a
profound impression or to sway the minds of
thinking men, and he never, except in the
" Federalist," worked under greater difficulties
nor with greater success than when he entered
the lists as " Camillus."

But when Hamilton first began to write the
clouds had gathered thick and black; it seemed
as if the popular rage would infallibly lead to
war, and, in order to make the position of the
President still more difficult, England, with her
customary stupidity, seized that moment to re-
new the obnoxious provision order. This gave
pain even to those most anxious for peace. To
Hamilton it seemed intolerable; to Washington
hardly to be endured. Outraged by the nation
with which he was seeking to make peace, with
his own party demoralized and hushed, and
with the opposition in full cry urging on the
popular clamor, the President faced the great
question. With that high, serene, silent courage which he always showed, whether in the
shock of unsuccessful battle or in the din of
hostile politics, Washington deliberated. He
would do his duty, — that was a matter of
course. As to what that duty was, he felt
but little doubt. But with the almost painful
sense of justice and responsibility which always

characterized him, Washington wished to know all sides. He consulted but few persons, and among those few Hamilton was first, as much so as if he had never left the cabinet. Hamilton on his side responded as fully and zealously as if he were still the President's secretary. He inclined to an attempt for further negotiation, and advised a refusal to exchange ratifications unless the provision order should be rescinded. On the general principle that the treaty, which meant peace on honorable if not on advantageous terms, was better than war, he sympathized with Washington. At Washington's request he drew up a summary of the arguments on both sides with that clearness in appreciating all points in a case which made him such a valued adviser to a man summoned to give a grave decision. He was disposed, on the whole, to be rather more aggressive and less sacrificing than Washington, as was natural to his temperament, but when the President finally acted, ratified the treaty, and sent it to England with a sharp remonstrance against the provision order, Hamilton fully sustained him. In all the struggle which followed in repelling attacks on the administration, and during the fierce contest over the treaty in the House, he played the same leading part. He was the trusted counselor of Washington, the adviser of the party leaders,

and the man to whom all the most active Federalists turned for suggestions, for arguments, and
for unfailing aid by tongue and pen, in letters
and through the press.

While Hamilton was occupying this important and influential position in the party and
before the country, the presidential election
came on. Washington had withdrawn from the
field, and the serious problem of selecting a candidate for the succession confronted the Federalists. They faced this question for the first
time, and on the result, as after events showed,
the fate of the party largely depended. There
were four men from whom the choice, as it
seemed at the time, must be made, — Hamilton,
Adams, Jay, and Thomas Pinckney of South
Carolina. Hamilton was the head of the Federalists, but he was the leader of the leaders
rather than of the party. He never had a strong
hold on the people, or on the rank and file even
of his own party. Moreover, he was the man
most hated and feared by the opposition. He
was the incarnation of the whole Federalist policy from the foundation of the government, and
as a candidate he would have aroused enmities
too fierce to have permitted his election. This
was plainly seen, and by no one more plainly
than by Hamilton himself, for there is no evidence that he ever gave the idea of securing the

Federalist nomination for the Presidency serious consideration, or was influenced by it for a
moment. Jay's name was so closely associated
with the conflict of the treaty as to put him, too,
out of the lists. Pinckney was well known and
popular, especially on account of the brilliant
success of his treaty with Spain, but he was a
new man and a Southerner, and the Federalist
strongholds were in the North. There remained
John Adams, who was, with the exception of
Hamilton, the most conspicuous man in the
party, and he had had a long and distinguished
career. He contended with Hamilton, also, for
the perilous honor of being the chief mark for
the concentrated dislike of the opposition. But
he was, on the other hand, still revered for eminent services in the Revolution, his name still
awakened the memories of the great conflict for
independence, and he had in this way a hold
upon the body of the party and upon the popular imagination. Moreover, he was a Northern
man and in the line of promotion.

It was therefore determined by the party leaders to vote for Adams and Pinckney for the first
and second offices respectively; a wise conclusion, which made what would, in the language
of to-day, be called a "strong ticket." Unfortunately the Constitution did not then admit of
a "ticket." The person receiving the highest

number of votes was President, the next highest Vice-President.   This opened the door to
an infinite amount of management and intrigue
in the electoral colleges.   The Federalists were
well aware that their chance of success was narrow, and that no votes could be spared.   Hamilton's views were simple enough.   He wished
first to hold the administration in the party, and
then to win the second place for a Federalist and
exclude Jefferson.   To do this he urged upon
all his friends the policy of voting strictly for
both Adams and Pinckney, and of throwing no
votes away.   In so doing he was right, clearly
and beyond all question, and the departure from
this policy elected Jefferson to the second place.
By its adoption two contingencies were possible:
either Adams and Pinckney would receive an
equal number of votes, which would throw the
decision into the House of Representatives, and
probably give the election to Adams; or — and
this was the hypothesis fatal to the scheme —
the South would throw away their votes for
Adams and make Pinckney President.   To this
latter contingency Hamilton was indifferent.
Indeed, it is pretty clear that he preferred
Pinckney, because he felt that he would then
continue to be the controlling influence with
the administration, while his observation had
led him to suspect that the reverse would prob-

ably be the case under Adams. In letting his preference for Pinckney, or rather his indifference of choice as between Pinckney and Adams, be known, Hamilton made a mistake. As the principal leader of the party he was bound to sink personal preferences and support the choice of the party for the first place without any reservation, and he should have put the plan of voting equally for both candidates solely on the ground of party success, treating the possible election of Pinckney as a thing never to be considered, much less viewed with indifference. How far Hamilton's position injured his own policy of voting it would now be difficult to say. The plan was doomed to defeat, because South Carolina would not vote for a Northern man, a fact of which New England, unluckily, was well aware. The result was that both sections threw away votes, electing Adams by a bare plurality of three, and defeating Pinckney, bringing about exactly the mischief Hamilton had striven so earnestly to prevent, the choice of Jefferson as Vice-President.

When Adams was inaugurated the situation was both novel and difficult. Adams, unlike Washington, was elected by a party and strictly as a party man. He was, by virtue of his office, head of the party *de jure*. But despite the President's hold upon the people, Hamilton, owing

to his brilliant services and his predominant influence with almost all the party leaders, was
the head of the Federalists *de facto*. On the
relations existing between these two men, therefore, the welfare of the party largely depended.
Both Adams and Hamilton were honestly anxious for the success of their party, for the well-
being and advancement of their country, and
for the maintenance of the cardinal principles
of Washington's administration. Unfortunately
they entered upon this new and trying period
in the career of their party with feelings of
coolness, if not of mutual distrust. Hamilton
had taken votes from Adams at the first election
to make sure that the selection of Washington
for the first place should not be endangered. In
the years which followed, Adams gave a sturdy
and often decisive support to the treasury measures and to the general policy of the administration, so that at the second election he received
Hamilton's hearty support for the vice-presidency, and their relations were then cordial. In
the third election Adams was aware of Hamilton's policy of equal voting, which he hastily
attributed to nothing but the latter's preference
for Pinckney. This revived the memory of the
first election, and Adams quickly set down the
whole thing as one long-continued and jealous
intrigue. Hamilton had erred at the first elec-

tion by taking doubtful action for which there
was no occasion. His policy at the last was
wise and right, but he made the mistake of not
burying his personal preferences and keeping
them out of sight.

When Adams came to the head of the government he regarded Hamilton as guilty of the
almost unpardonable sin of want of respect
toward himself, as prone to intrigue, grasping,
dictatorial, and of great power in the party.
Hamilton, on his side, thought Adams unreasonable, unmanageable, at times wrong-headed, in
short unsafe; and he had unfortunately been at
very little pains in the recent past to conceal
these opinions. Hamilton had gone out of office
in good faith and he had no desire to regain it,
but he had a profound interest in the fate of the
Federalist policy which had made the Union,
and which was so largely the work of his own
hands. He, therefore, was anxious to retain
his influence with the administration and his
power in the party. His position entitled him
to confidence and consultation, and he was by
no means a difficult counselor, nor anxious to
absorb all credit to himself. If the work was
well done, Hamilton cared little who did it.
When on one or two occasions he grasped at the
ensigns of command, it was because he honestly
believed that he was the only man fit to bear

their weight.   He was a severe and penetrating
critic, but neither jealous nor captious.   It was
perfectly easy to manage Hamilton and win his
cordial support.   Washington had never found
the slightest difficulty in dealing with him in or
out of office.   All that was required was tact,
full and frank consultation, and the deference to
which his opinions were on every ground entitled.

Tact in managing men, however, was conspicuous in John Adams chiefly by its absence.
Fear did not enter into his composition, and he
was sure to do what he believed to be right at
all hazards, but he could not be right gracefully
and with address.   Every dictate of prudence
and of party obligation bound him to consult
Hamilton, and yet he undertook to ignore him
first and crush him afterwards.   Hamilton, on
his part, when he found that the President was
prejudiced against him, and bolted wildly at the
thought of being influenced by him, should have
supported the administration when he could,
and, if his advice openly offered was neglected,
should have remained passive so long as he
could consistently remain in the party.   This
would have been not only wise, but dignified
and in keeping with his position, and it would
not have concealed his opinions or diminished
their due weight with the party at large.   Unfortunately such a course required very great

self - control, which was difficult to Hamilton's
imperious and energetic nature. Instead of
either leaving Mr. Adams alone or openly resisting him in the party, he undertook to force
the President's hand, through his power over
the cabinet and the leaders in Congress. The
result of such relations between these two chiefs
was certain to cause an open breach as soon as
they differed in policy, and equally sure to produce disaster to the party.

Washington had settled the English question. Danger in that quarter was removed, and
the means employed to effect the removal were
one fruitful cause of peril in another direction.
In proportion as our relations with England
improved, those with France grew worse. Mr.
Monroe, after a career of light-headed mischief
unparalleled in our diplomatic history, had
finally been recalled from France. Mr. Charles
Cotesworth Pinckney had been sent in his stead,
and had been refused a reception. With matters in this state, and on the heels of a savage
controversy with the French minister, Mr. Adams
took the helm. The country was again on the
verge of war, and the first question which confronted the administration was the settlement of
this difficulty. The question was, whether we
should stand upon our dignity and prepare at
once for war, or make another effort for peace.

The decision of this question brought to light the existence of a third faction which agreed neither with Hamilton nor Adams, although in general sympathy with the former. Its representative and most active leader was Colonel Pickering, the secretary of state, and it found its principal support among the Federalists of New England. Hamilton regarded the French republic with unqualified dislike and distrust. He believed that the war they were then waging was directed against everything he held most precious, against constitutional liberty, law, order, and society. At the same time he was too much of a statesman not to perceive that war ought to be avoided by us if it was possible, and that the policy which he had advocated with reference to England should also be pursued toward France. The cabinet faction, going beyond Hamilton in their hatred of French principles, believed that the sooner we were committed to open hostilities with the great republic, and all that it represented, the better. Adams, however, took the same view as Hamilton, and the policy of sending three special peace commissioners prevailed. Before the force of the united opinion of the two chief leaders all factions were powerless, and this shows only too plainly the terrible blunder made by Adams in not making it his first object to consult with Hamilton, and act in conjunction with him. So far all went well; but on the composition of the commission, which was of deep political importance in any event, and which in case of war was sure to be of the greatest moment in its effect upon public opinion, Adams and Hamilton parted company.

All were agreed that Pinckney must be one of the three commissioners, and that the commission ought to consist of two Federalists and one Democrat. Pinckney represented the South, and Hamilton wished that the other Federalist should be taken from the North, and that the Democrat should be Madison or even Jefferson, — in other words a leading Virginian and Democrat who was widely known and personally respected by all parties, a "character," as Hamilton expressed it, "in whom France and the opposition had full reliance." Adams, carried away by the suspicion that an attempt was being made to force upon him a nomination from the Hamiltonian faction in New England, took Marshall, from Virginia, and Gerry, as the Democrat, from Massachusetts. To take both Federalists from the South, where the party had no strength, was hardly wise, but to take a northern Democrat in place of Madison, especially a man of Gerry's slender abilities, was a most serious blunder. Gerry brought discredit on the mission by his weakness and over-confidence, and produced a good deal of mischief, although it may be questioned whether he affected materially the general result. His appointment was not only a poor one in itself, but it had a bad effect at home, exasperated the feeling in certain quarters against the President, was generally considered injudicious, and caused Adams much subsequent annoyance. The general policy of Washington's time was, however, maintained. As in the case of Jay, Hamilton was for very stiff instructions, at first almost unreasonably so, and, as in the former instance, milder counsels prevailed, and the envoys went forth upon their mission.

The result is well known. The commissioners were insulted and outraged in every possible way. They were improperly received; and when attempts to bully and bribe had failed to sway them, they were driven from France. To the opposition clamoring for information about the negotiation with their beloved France, Mr. Adams sent in the famous X. Y. Z. correspondence. The mixture of swindling and browbeating thus disclosed, heightened as it was by news of a decree far surpassing its predecessors in defiance of neutral rights, and by the burning of one of our vessels by a French privateer, lighted up a hot flame of indignation which swept rapidly and fiercely over the country, setting it ablaze with the spirit of war.

This exposure utterly discredited also the
party of the opposition friendly to France and
broke them down completely. One by one they
slipped away from Congress, where they had
a majority, leaving the undaunted Gallatin to
face not merely defeat, but what seemed to be
disgrace. Jefferson, with a discomfited whine,
bowed before the storm, and even Giles is said
for the moment to have lost a little of his usual
rough effrontery. With the Federalists, of
course, everything was just the reverse. Enthusiastic addresses poured in upon the President,
who responded to them with equal fervor, and
in a most spirited manner. In the press, and at
public meetings, men rivaled each other in denunciation of France. War vessels were fitted
out by private subscription and presented to the
government; and Marshall, returning to be received with fêtes and banquets, raised the public wrath to a still higher pitch. The Federalists carried rapidly all the strong measures of
defense which they deemed essential, — a provisional army and an increase of troops, of fortifi-
cations, and of the navy. At the next general
election they triumphed, and found themselves
in possession for the first time of a strong majority. The conduct of France raised them to
the zenith of their power, but it was of short
duration, and their strength brought with it the

events which reduced them soon after to utter
ruin. The first result was the fight made by the
President against the appointment of Hamilton
to the command of the provisional army.

Washington was selected as commander-in-
chief, and consented to serve, provided he should
not take an active part until the army should
be actually in the field, and provided further
that he should have the choice of the officers
who were to be next him in rank and to act as
his staff. Washington was clearly of opinion
that the army ought to be constituted *de novo*,
and that there should be no question of revolutionary rank. He accordingly sent to the President a list of major-generals, in the following
order: Hamilton, Charles Cotesworth Pinckney,
and Knox. This gave the practical command
and the work of organization to Hamilton. Mr.
Adams sent Washington's name at once to the
Senate, and then the major - generals in the
order prescribed by Washington. This done,
he wheeled about when it came to signing the
commissions, and took the ground that Knox
was the senior officer on account of his revolutionary rank. He disregarded the fact that, by
the precedents of the Congress of the confederacy, officers ranked in the order of their confirmation. He refused to admit that Hamilton was
the man best fitted for the post, and was so con-

sidered by the public; he plunged himself and
his party into a bitter personal quarrel, and all
because he disliked Hamilton, and was enraged
at the opposition of the cabinet to himself.

The President's course led to an immediate
and desperate struggle. Not only the cabinet,
but all the leading Federalists, urged upon him
the adoption of Washington's list. He alienated Knox from Hamilton, who was a friend of
long standing, and ultimately caused the former's resignation, while Pinckney on his return
fully admitted the propriety of the appoint-
ments, and cheerfully took service in the rank
assigned by Washington. The pressure of opinion upon the President grew stronger constantly,
and yet, though he writhed a good deal in anger,
he seemed to become more fixed in his purpose. The Federalist leaders, deeply alarmed,
turned to Mount Vernon for assistance. In un-
mistakable language Washington told Adams
that if the agreement made between them was
not adhered to he should resign. Adams was
a bold and stubborn man, but he dared not face
the displeasure of Washington and the consequences of his resignation on such a question.
In bitterness of spirit he gave way, and appointed Hamilton to the first place, and the
sense of defeat changed keen dislike to an almost
venomous hatred of the man whom he chose to

think his rival. The conduct of Adams in this
whole affair is utterly indefensible. There is
not a single valid reason for the course he took.
From a personal feeling he brought on a bitter,
senseless, and perfectly futile quarrel, weakened
the party and himself, and all because he disliked the man who happened to be best fitted for
the command of the army. No adverse criticism can be made upon Hamilton, except that,
while at first he quietly accepted the situation
to which he was called by Washington and the
party, after the contest over his appointment
began, he exhibited a rather disagreeable and
aggressive self-assertion common enough in men
of great abilities and commanding wills, and
from which he was on rare occasions not wholly
free. Thus the appointment was finally made,
leaving a legacy of heart-burning, a memory of
compulsion and defeat on one side, and of injustice and triumph on the other.

With his accustomed zeal, Hamilton at once
threw himself into his new work, and gave himself up to it heart and soul. His task was that
of organization and preparation, for which he
had a peculiar genius, and it is needless to say
that his work was of the best. He was first
called upon to draft a plan for the fortification
of the harbor of New York and superintend its
execution, funds having been appropriated by

the State for that purpose.   This was somewhat
outside the regular path of his duty, but he gave
it his attention and made the necessary arrangements.   Soon after, he met Washington and
Pinckney at Philadelphia and drew up a scheme
which Washington adopted for the apportion-
ment of officers and men among the States, for
a recruiting system, and for supplies, arsenals,
camp equipages, and ordnance.   In a second
paper, likewise accepted by Washington, he laid
out a plan for the organization of the army, in
which he dealt with the questions of pay, uni-
forms, rations, rank, promotion, field exercise,
regulation of barracks, the police of garrisons
and camps, and the issue of arms, clothing, and
fuel.   These elaborate suggestions were necessarily hasty, but they exhibit great familiarity
with the various subjects, fertility of resource,
and broad and comprehensive views.   They received the highest proof of their value in gain-
ing the approval of Washington, the best and
most experienced soldier of the day.

When Congress assembled, Hamilton sent to
the Senate a bill which became law and was entitled, " An Act for the better organizing of the
troops of the United States."   This measure
changed as little as possible the existing system,
dealing chiefly with the proportion to be established between the number of officers and of

men. Hamilton's purpose was to make a " fundamental arrangement," so that in the future the existing system could be increased or diminished at will without altering the form of organization. He also drafted a bill for a " Medical Establishment," and devised plans for the classification and organization of the militia, for trade with the Indians, and for military supplies, and from time to time he issued circulars to the army to check intemperance, dueling, and desertion, and to promote discipline. McHenry, in fact, turned to Hamilton for instructions on every point connected with the War Department, while Stoddert and Wolcott sought his advice in an almost equal degree as to the policy to be pursued with regard to the navy and the treasury. In the spring of 1799 he made every necessary arrangement for the invasion of Louisiana and the Floridas. He also prepared a scheme for the establishment and maintenance of frontier posts, and devoted much time and attention to the fortification of New York. Hamilton's bills for organization, for the medical establishment, and for the eventual augmentation of the army, all became laws, but the work of actual recruiting was constantly delayed, until at last, after the departure of the second peace commission, it became obvious that there would be no war, and all active measures gradually ceased. Hamilton's military services at this time went no farther than the elaboration of plans and the work of preparation; the only lasting result of his labors being the establishment of the West Point Academy a few years later in general conformity with his suggestions. Hamilton in all these matters exhibited, however, not only his usual energetic and indefatigable industry and his readiness in dealing with a wide range of topics, but he showed that he possessed in a high degree the military attributes of foresight, breadth of view, knowledge of details, and great capacity for organization. Whether if he had been called into actual service he would have displayed in equal measure the still more important qualities which are essential to a successful general in an active campaign and on the field of battle, must remain mere conjecture. This much is certain, that he did the best that was possible in all that fell to him to do, and that his strong hand was felt in all departments of the government in regard to everything relating to the war policy of the United States.

But while Hamilton was devoting himself to these laborious duties, he was working out in his usual manner detailed and comprehensive plans for the general conduct of the war. He saw that there would be no battles to fight with

France in the East, and he was convinced that
the only way to reach her was through the sides
of her ally, Spain. He therefore designed to
wrest from the latter power the region of the
extreme Southwest, and give to the United
States final and complete control of the great
valley of the Mississippi. These ideas were of
long standing, and were part of that conception
of nationality and of national greatness which
was the predominating influence in Hamilton's
public career. The last resolution which he had
introduced in the Congress of the Confederation
declared the " navigation of the Mississippi to
be a clear and essential right and to be supported as such." A few years later he had said
in the cabinet that the free use of that river was
" essential to the unity of the empire." In 1798
he urged upon Pickering the necessity of getting
possession of Louisiana and the Floridas, and in
the following year he wrote: " I have been long
in the habit of considering the acquisition of
those countries as essential to the permanency
of the Union."

It seemed now as if the moment had come
when these theories might be put into execution,
and it is no wonder that they were uppermost
in Hamilton's thoughts. Both from a political
and military point of view he was right. The
national and imperial instincts of his nature did

not mislead him. The Mississippi and the great regions of the Southwest were essential to union and empire. The future has justified him, and in no single point has it shown more strikingly the range of Hamilton's vision as a statesman and the force and penetration of his mind. By one of the strange but not uncommon contradictions which we meet with in human history, it fell to the lot of Hamilton's keenest foe to carry out the most imperial part of the great Federalist's national policy. It was reserved to Jefferson to acquire by purchase, and in what was then thought to be defiance of the Constitution, the vast territory which Hamilton planned only a few years before to win by arms. The accomplishment of the work fell to other hands, but the conception was Hamilton's, and it was he who first formulated the brilliant scheme, and after years of waiting devised means which would have assured success.

Besides the control of the Mississippi and the conquest of the Southwest there had long been in Hamilton's mind still another idea which, while national in its origin, was intended rather to increase the power of the United States than to strengthen their union. "Our situation," he wrote in "The Federalist," "invites, and our situation prompts us to aim at an ascendant in American affairs." We were to be dominant

in the western hemisphere. We were not only
to be neutral as to the affairs of Europe, but
we were to exact from Europe neutrality in all
regarding America, and were to crush out European influence. Here is the Monroe doctrine
in its widest scope, and with such notions long
cherished, and while he was revolving these plans
for the acquisition of Louisiana, it is no wonder
that Hamilton's imagination was touched by the
schemes of the Spanish adventurer Miranda.
He began to believe that the time had come for
conquests beyond the Mississippi which should
result in the liberation of the Central and even
of the South American States, and in the establishment of republics in those regions.

Miranda had been long engaged in these
schemes, and had already endeavored to enlist
England as an ally. He now wished to have
England and the United States unite and un-
dertake the overthrow of the Spanish power in
South America. This fell in with the Federalist longing to join all decent people in a cru-
sade against the hated French republic. Such
an alliance would insure the ruin of Spain, the
tool of France, the closing of the South American ports to French privateers, and great acquisition of territory to the United States. It was,
in case of war with France, both a wise and
sufficiently practicable policy, and it is no won-

der that Hamilton thought it worth consideration by the government, and at all events judged
that it was well to be informed as to the progress of such a movement. He therefore sought
to interest the government in Miranda, and no
doubt gave undue importance to that soldier of
fortune; but his own campaign was that of a
great general and a far-seeing statesman. Military glory appealed strongly to a sweeping
intellect and powerful nature like Hamilton's,
and we may readily believe that he dreamed of
extensive conquests and great deeds of arms.
That he thought the opportunity likely to come
at that moment is more than doubtful. It is
certain that it never affected his public course,
and that he never aimed at anything which,
however it might redound to his own fame,
went beyond an extension and consolidation of
the power of the United States. The theory
that his mind teemed with visions of empire and
of military power in the Napoleonic fashion,
schemes fraught with danger and perhaps despotism, is due to the heated and hostile mind of
Mr. Adams. Hamilton was not only extremely
guarded in his correspondence with Miranda, to
whom he said that " he could personally have
no participation in his plan unless patronized
by the government of the United States," but he
was also in consultation with Rufus King, our

cautious minister to England. Throughout he
scrupulously avoided doing or saying anything
which could by any possibility give ground for
the suspicion that he was taking part in the
schemes of an adventurer without the assent
of his government. The plan appealed to his
strongest instincts as a statesman and soldier,
and fired his imagination. It was, too, not unreasonable, and in the event of war Hamilton
determined to be in a position to take every
advantage of such brilliant possibilities.

But while Hamilton gave himself up to the
onerous duties immediately before him, his
dreams and aspirations, if he had any, came to
a speedy end. The popular indignation and the
hearty support of the administration, the bold
attitude of the United States, and the fighting
qualities of our little navy, already striking telling blows at the French privateers and men-of-
war, all impressed France with the fact that she
had aroused a nation out of reach of her armies,
and capable of becoming a very formidable ad-
versary. The worthy Talleyrand accordingly
began to cast about for some means by which
he could reëstablish friendly relations, at the
lowest possible cost to the pockets and the feelings of the French people and of himself. By
circuitous channels, but in direct terms, he conveyed to Mr. Adams the fact that the govern-

ment would be glad to receive an American envoy with all the respect and honor to which he was entitled. Acting on this information, and without a word to any one, not even to his cabinet, the President sent in the nomination of Mr. Vans Murray to be minister to France.

There can be no doubt that honorable peace was then, as in Washington's time, the paramount consideration. Whether it was wise to snap at the very first opportunity held out by France is more questionable. John Adams certainly believed it to be so, but his haste, secrecy, and the abrupt change from his recent utterances, make it impossible not to suppose that one strong motive for this sudden action was to be found in his belief that peace would cripple the war party, including Hamilton, and all others who differed with him. But admitting that John Adams was not only right in principle, but also in the selection of the moment for making peace, yet his mode of doing right was utterly and hopelessly wrong. If his cabinet agreed with him, then concealment was useless ; if they were certain to oppose him, then concealment may have been shrewd and cunning, but it was neither very wise nor very brave. In any event, it rent asunder hopelessly the already distracted Federalists. It fell upon the unsuspecting party with the suddenness of a bolt of lightning. They were stunned by the shock, and their first thought was to defeat the President in the Senate, and to break down his policy and him together. These were the views of men who believed a war with France to be a good thing in itself, because it was the only sure salvation from the pestilent ideas of Paris. They would have had us ally ourselves with England, because it behooved all decent people throughout the world to stand together and stamp out the monstrous doctrines of the French Revolution.

No man hated those doctrines and principles more fervently than Hamilton, and no one sacrificed more than he to opposition to the propaganda of unbridled democracy and consequent anarchy. But, except on one or two occasions, the statesman always prevailed with Hamilton. Except in the case of a common war against France when the results would bring vast and immediate benefits to the United States, he had no mind for an alliance with England, much as he applauded her as the defender of society. He was, on the contrary, disposed to be cool toward her because, with a stupidity really exquisite, she had begun, just as we were embroiled with France, once more to annoy and provoke us with outrageous orders in council. Hamilton's general policy, therefore, was the maintenance of a strong dignified attitude, backed by armed men and ships, and then a quiet waiting until France should come to her senses and send a minister to us. He never believed war to be a good thing in itself, as did some of his more extreme partisans, who were as headstrong and unruly in their way as the President was in his; but he regarded peace now and always as the first object. In this he was not only wise but consistent with his past. At the same time the sudden change of Adams, his eager grasp at the earliest symptom of returning decency in the French government, disappointed and angered Hamilton as a hasty, needless step, and an un-called-for sacrifice of a dignity which might have been scrupulously maintained and much enhanced without endangering a speedy and lasting peace. His wrath was still further kindled by the foolish and offensive method of action adopted by the President.

But even in bitterness and anger the states-man was still uppermost. Hamilton may not have been the idol of the masses, nor a skillful manager of men; but there was one set of men whom he knew thoroughly, and those were the leaders of his own party. He knew them to be capable of becoming very dangerous, and he saw them now on the point of rising upon the President and beating him and the party to the

earth together. Checking his own feelings, but
without attempting to conceal his indignation,
he took the ground with the Federalists at
Philadelphia, that peace with honor was now,
as always, our first object, and that this step
toward it, however unwisely it had been taken,
was nevertheless beyond recall. The true policy
now was to make the best of what had been
done, and treat for peace as it should be treated
for. To send Murray alone was absurd ; it was
the idea of a man blinded with haste and anger.
Let a suitable commission be chosen and sent,
if circumstances still continued favorable. The
party leaders fell in with Hamilton's views, and,
Adams himself becoming aware of the error
of committing this charge to Murray alone,
a strong commission was nominated and confirmed. It is hardly too much to say that
Hamilton's prompt decision, his wisdom and
statesmanship, saved the party at this moment
from an immediate wreck, which he might very
readily and naturally have precipitated.

There was some delay in sending the commissioners, owing to the unsettled state of France,
and then came another revolution, which led
the Federalists to believe that there ought to
be a further suspension of the embassy. Hamilton even went to Trenton to urge delay ; but
Adams, irritated beyond endurance by the stub-

born and exasperating resistance of the war
party, as represented by his secretaries, treated
counsel and opposition alike with contempt, and
ordered the envoys away. Thus ended the first
great struggle over our relations with France.
Taken as a whole, from the arrival of Genet
to the departure of this last commission which
effected a treaty, the Federalist policy had been
a masterpiece at once bold and sagacious, and
one from which the country reaped great and
lasting benefit. But behind the fair exterior
of success was the triumphant party torn with
bitter dissensions, which were sapping its life
even in the moment of victory.

In another direction the policy of the Federalists, although giving rise to no quarrels, but
meeting, on the contrary, with general approval
in the party, became the most efficient cause of
their subsequent ruin. The publication of the
X. Y. Z. letters, and the flight of members of
the opposition from the House of Representatives, left absolute control with the Federalists.
They had been accustomed to winning battle
after battle, but they had always been in the
minority, and the want of numbers was a severe
and wholesome discipline which cultivated in
that party a prudence to which by nature they
were not much given. An absolute majority
and the irresistible rise of public opinion against

France turned their heads. They did not lose
their wits, but they became more masterful and
overbearing than ever. They rapidly pushed
through bills for an army, a navy, and fortifica-
tions, as well as a naturalization law which required fourteen years' residence, many of them
urging the refusal of citizenship to foreigners
altogether. So far no harm had been done; but
they next resolved to strike at the vile libels
which had been poured forth by the opposition
press upon Washington, and upon every other
honored name, and at the foreigners who wrote
the libels or propagated French doctrines and
set agitation on foot. With this object they en-
acted the famous Alien and Sedition laws. In
their first draft these laws were intolerable.
The Federalists in Congress were guided by the
members of the extreme war party, and were
now in a very rash mood, so that Hamilton was
much alarmed by these bills, and wrote urgently
in favor of modifications. Of the Alien Act,
and the mode of its execution, he said, " Let us
not be cruel or violent." In the first draft of
the Sedition Act he saw danger of civil war, and
said: " Let us not establish a tyranny. Energy
is a very different thing from violence." This
was the language of a statesman. But when
the laws were modified and passed, they and the
principles which they involved received Hamilton's entire support.

There has been a general effort on the part
of biographers to clear their respective heroes
from all responsibility for these ill-fated measures. The truth is, that they had the full
support of the congressmen and senators who
passed them, of the President who signed them,
and of the leaders in the States, who almost all
believed in them; and they also met with very
general acceptance by the party in the North.
Hamilton went as far in the direction of sus-
taining the principle of these laws as any one.
He had too acute a mind to believe, with many
of the stanch Federalist divines of New England, that Jefferson and Madison were Marats
and Robespierres, and that their followers were
Jacobins, who, when they came to power, were
ready for the overthrow of religion and society, and were prepared to set up a guillotine
and pour out blood in the waste places of the
federal city. But he did believe, and so wrote
to Washington, after the appearance of the
X. Y. Z. letters, that there was a party in the
country ready to " new model " the Constitution
on French principles, to form an offensive and
defensive alliance with France, and make the
United States a French province. He felt, in
short, that there was a party in America ready
for confiscation and social confusion. A year
later, in 1799, he wrote to Dayton, the speaker

of the national House of Representatives, a long
letter, in which he set forth very clearly the
policy which he felt ought to be pursued. He
wished to give strength to the government, and
increase centralization by every means, by an
extension of the national judiciary, a liberal
system of internal improvements, an increased
and abundant revenue, an enlargement of the
army and navy, permanence in the laws for the
volunteer army, extension of the powers of the
general government, subdivision of the States
as soon as practicable, and finally a strong sedition law, and the power to banish aliens. This
was what was termed at that day a "strong
and spirited" policy; it would now be called repressive; but by whatever name it is designated,
it was the policy of Hamilton, and is characteristic of both his talents and temperament.
Except as to the subdivision of States, it was
carried out pretty thoroughly in all its main
features by the Federalists.

The Alien and Sedition laws, although resisted
in Congress, did not much affect public opinion
at the elections which immediately ensued, and
the Federalists came into the next Congress
with a large majority. Numbers, however,
availed them little. In the worst days of their
minority period they were more effective as a
party. The jealousies and quarrels already on

foot came to a fierce culmination on the appointment of the second mission to France. The
moderate Federalists of the South, headed by
Marshall, sustained the President, while the war
party urged his destruction. It was a house
divided against itself, and at a time when violent
measures had so lessened the great advantages
of the last election that the Federalists entered
upon the presidential campaign with but a narrow margin for success. Jefferson sounded the
alarm in the famous Kentucky resolutions. The
doctrine was bad enough, but it was probably
merely intended to attract attention to the rapid
development of power on the part of the central
government. The resolutions of both Kentucky
and Virginia were received with little favor
anywhere, and in many States with strong and
formal reprobation. Hamilton, more deeply
stirred by a movement for disunion than he
could be by anything else, regarded these resolutions as of great gravity, and urged that they
be formally disapproved by Congress and their
evil tendencies fully displayed.

Jefferson, however, had achieved his purpose.
The suspicions of the country were awakened
to the meaning and possible results of such
legislation as the Alien and Sedition acts, and
to the centralizing policy of the Federalists.
The approach of peace, moreover, relaxed the

spirit which had rallied the masses to the side of
the Federalists as the defenders of the national
honor. Slowly, but surely, the dominant party
was losing ground in public opinion. Pennsylvania slipped from them at the state election,
and this made a victory in New York of the
very last importance. Hamilton threw himself
into the struggle with an energy and fire great
even for him. But he was now opposed to one
who was the first and by no means the least
in a long list of men, some of great ability and
distinction, who have risen to power and place
chiefly by capacity for guiding the dark and
complicated intrigues of New York politics. In
these Aaron Burr was a master. The election
turned largely on the result in the city, and in
ward politics Hamilton was no match for his
antagonist. Hamilton could neither trade, bargain, nor deal with petty factions. Such work
was unworthy of his powerful intellect, and the
sacrifice did not even bring the poor reward of
success. With voice and pen Hamilton maintained the conflict. His eloquence was unrivaled, his arguments, written and spoken, were
unanswerable, but Burr had the votes. New
York was lost to the Federalists and ruin stared
them in the face.

In the bitterness and passion of defeat Hamilton proposed to Governor Jay to call together

the old legislature and give the choice of presidential electors to districts, thus dividing the vote of New York, which would otherwise be settled by the incoming legislature, who would choose none but Democrats. Jay very frankly declined to consider the scheme, as one wholly improper. The proposition was, in fact, nothing less than to commit, under the forms of law, a fraud, which would set aside the expressed will of a majority of the voters in the State. This is the one dark blot upon the public career of Hamilton. It is no palliation to say that he was urged to it by the Federalist members of Congress. The error of a great leader cannot be excused by saying that lesser men advised him to it. Many times before Hamilton had stepped in boldly and had effectually checked the rash and headstrong impulses of his more extreme friends at Philadelphia. He now fell in with them in support of this high-handed measure. It was he who advised it with Jay, it was he who urged its prosecution, and on his shoulders must rest the responsibility. Hamilton was too clear-sighted even then to attempt to disguise the character of the scheme. He says plainly to Jay, we must not be "over-scrupulous," and then adduces a great many lucid and ingenious reasons to show that this is a time when to do a great right one is justified in doing a little wrong. Arguments on that side of the question were not wanting; they never are to the champions of order, the saviors of society, the "strong men," and the imperialists of this world. That Hamilton was carried away by a passion of disappointment when he wrote this letter is no doubt true, but the root of the matter lay still deeper. The bitterness of defeat and the readiness to use violent means to recover lost ground sprang from the belief, fostered and developed in Hamilton's mind by the French Revolution, that there was a party in this country of democracy, license, and anarchy, that its victory meant ruin to the state, and that salvation could only be assured by the continuance in power of the party of order and Federalism. This frame of mind is not uncommon in the history of party conflicts, but in the days of the " Great Monster," as Hamilton called the French Republic, it was intensified to a degree and carried to an extent hardly ever known before or since. That this dread of the success of the other side in a representative government should have led such a man as Hamilton to make a proposition like that contained in the letter to Jay, is a most melancholy example of the power and the danger of such sentiments, which are wholly foreign to free constitutional systems.

But even while the fortunes of the party were thus declining, they were hurried still faster on their downward course by the ever-increasing bitterness and the greater openness of the quarrels among the leaders. The nomination of the peace commission led to violent attacks upon the President by Pickering, who seems to have resolved to break him down, and these attacks, made in private letters, were now circulated with but little pretense of secrecy among the New England leaders. Immediately after the New York election, which crippled Hamilton by depriving him of the control of the vote of that State in the electoral college, Adams drove McHenry and Pickering from his cabinet. This deepened the feud, and Adams, irritated by the assaults of his opponents, gave loose to his own tongue, at all times a rather unruly member. Among other abusive things, he called his opponents a British faction, and stigmatized Hamilton, in particular, as acting in the interests of England. This attack soon reached Hamilton's ears, and in view of its source he felt that it could not be passed over in silence. He accordingly wrote a brief note, stating that he had heard the reported accusation of the President, and inquiring if the report were true. Receiving no reply he again wrote to Mr. Adams, repeating his question and denying the truth of

the alleged charge. Both notes were courteous
and straightforward, but they were passed over
in complete silence. It must not be forgotten
that there was no open breach between the President and Hamilton. Their relations were as
yet friendly, in form at least. Moreover, only
a short time before, Mr. Adams had written
to Hamilton asking his assistance in securing
for Colonel Smith, the President's son-in-law, a
desirable position in the army. Hamilton had
cheerfully and generously given his services, and
his note was pleasant and friendly. Yet, with
this incident fresh in his mind, Mr. Adams did
not hesitate to refuse to notice a proper and
reasonable question asked by the principal officer of the army, who was also one of the most
distinguished men in the country. To say that
such treatment on the part of Mr. Adams was
uncivil, is but little. It was a gross blunder,
and was unfortunately of a piece with all Mr.
Adams's conduct towards Hamilton. When the
latter came to Trenton to urge the suspension
of the peace commission, Mr. Adams referred to
his visit with a pitying sneer. Hamilton was
the most powerful leader of the Federalists; he
was the most conspicuous and brilliant statesman in the country; and yet the President, the
head of the Federalist party, first undertook to
ignore him, then slighted his advice and derided

him, and finally treated his manly inquiry with
contemptuous silence. Decency, prudence, and
self-interest, to take no higher motives, dictated
an opposite course. I am very far from holding
Mr. Adams solely responsible for the downfall
of the Federalists, but his treatment of Hamilton, tried merely by the test of statesmanship and good politics, shows how completely he
failed as a leader of men, and how he became,
despite all his courage, honesty, and abilities, a
principal cause in the ruin of the party.

Quarrels like these could not long be confined
to the knowledge of the leaders. They were
sure to break out and, coming to the surface before the public, to work all the vast mischief of
which they were capable. They reached their
height just as the presidential election drew
near. To throw Adams over meant an open
split and certain defeat, and the leaders in Congress with much misgiving, and on the part of
many with no great good-will, resolved to support him again as a candidate for the presidency, in conjunction with Charles Cotesworth
Pinckney for Vice-President. Hamilton made
the best of what seemed to him a very bad
business. Even after the loss of New York,
there was still a chance for the Federalists if
South Carolina would vote for both candidates.
Hamilton urged, therefore, once more, an equal

vote for both Pinckney and Adams, and again
it may be said that his policy was the only one
which could have secured success.   It was generally supposed, however, that this course would
result in the election of Pinckney, a result which
Hamilton openly preferred.   It was bad enough
to have this preference for Pinckney generally
known; but Hamilton was now so thoroughly
enraged and so completely alienated from the
President that he went still farther and wrote a
pamphlet designed to show up Mr. Adams's failings, and to vindicate his own position and that
of the war Federalists.

The project was so utterly wild that every
effort was made to dissuade Hamilton from his
purpose.   The disapprobation, indeed, was so
general that even he resolved at the last moment to limit the circulation of this effusion
to a few friends.   But it was too late.   Burr,
through his agents, stole a copy, and the pamphlet appeared.   This famous production is a
defense of the war Federalists and a personal
attack on Mr. Adams.   A good deal of the censure was just enough, but the pamphlet as a
whole was a piece of passionate folly.   Hamilton
denounced as unsafe, violent, vain, and egotistic,
a Federalist President whose general public policy all Federalists supported; and then wound
up his bitter diatribe with the lame and impo-

tent conclusion of advising every one to vote for
the man so much to be distrusted.   The whole
thing was simple self-stultification, and the pamphlet met with no favor except among the Democrats.   Even Hamilton's closest friends were
frightened and displeased.   If the Federalists
had openly divided, and the two wings had engaged in controversy, a polemic of this sort might
have seemed natural.   But for one great leader
to publish such an attack upon another, when
the party was formally in harmony and upon
the eve of a close and doubtful contest for the
presidency, was simple madness.   It was the
work of a man crazed with passion and bent on
revenge.

This unhappy incident cannot be dismissed
without a word upon Hamilton's relations with
the cabinet.   It has been charged that in this
respect he acted in bad faith.   That the cabinet officers went too far in furnishing Hamilton,
and others also, with all sorts of information
which came to them in a confidential capacity,
will not, I think, be questioned.   It is not apparent, however, that Hamilton made any improper use of this information; for although
he was anxious enough for material, there was
none to be had which was of peculiar value or
novelty.   But there is no ground for accusing
Hamilton of bad faith in this particular.   He

made a mistake in trying, through his influence
with the cabinet, to force the President's hand;
but he had a perfect right, as a party leader,
to correspond with the secretaries, and to give
them his opinions and advice on political questions. He had done the same thing in Washington's time, and no one has ever hinted that
there was any impropriety in it. The fact that
he was not personally on good terms with Adams does not affect the matter. Hamilton was
fully entitled to write private letters to members
of the cabinet, and they had a right to receive
them. The fact that the secretaries, after they
found themselves in opposition to the President,
ought to have retired, is a wholly distinct matter, and must be discussed on different grounds.
If they chose to be guided by Hamilton, a private individual and unofficial leader, that was
their affair, not his. The pamphlet against
Adams was passionate, foolish, and contradictory
in itself, and it placed Hamilton in a weak and
false position, but it was an open attack, and
was not liable to the charge of bad faith.

If anything was needed to make the overthrow of the Federalists certain, this unfortunate pamphlet would have done it. But the
party's doom was already sealed. South Carolina would vote only for a Southern man, and
Pinckney, with the chivalrous sense of duty

which he always displayed, refused to be separated from Adams. The result was the defeat of the candidates of the Federalists, and the close of their party career as rulers of national politics. The struggle of the election did not, however, come to an end in the electoral colleges. The equal vote received by Burr and Jefferson threw the final decision into the House of Representatives, and the former began at once to sound his way toward an arrangement which should bring him in as president over Jefferson. The Federalists in Congress, maddened and reckless by defeat, turned with avidity to the chance of snatching the office from their arch-enemy Jefferson. The crisis was very grave, and indeed threatened civil war. Once more the Federalists at Washington were running to perilous extremes, and once more Hamilton checked them. The wild passion which had led him into the attack on Adams had spent itself, and he was again the cool, wise, far-seeing statesman with his prejudices and impulses under the control of reason. He knew that Jefferson was the fairly chosen President, and that such was the intention of the people. He saw the danger which setting Jefferson aside by an intrigue would bring. Much as he disliked the man, he knew that his former colleague was timid, cautious, and trained in politics of the better sort. He also knew Burr, and rightly believed the hero of New York city politics to be shallow, dangerous, and utterly unscrupulous. Putting aside all personal feeling, he threw himself into the conflict and exerted his powerful influence to check the mad projects of the Federalists. His intervention probably had a decisive effect. It was certainly courageous, highminded, and such as became the distinguished leader of a great party. After the storm of the election and the bitterness of party faction, it was a fit conclusion to Hamilton's career as a public man, which practically ended with the downfall of his party.

CHAPTER X

PROFESSIONAL LIFE — DUEL AND DEATH

THE defeat of the Federalists left Hamilton wholly free to devote himself to the practice of the law. Fortunately for him, his work was something very different from the merely nominal occupation which retired statesmen and disappointed politicians sometimes dignify by the name of "their profession." The proscriptive laws against Tories, as has been said, had given to Hamilton, Burr, and a few others complete possession of the New York practice after the Revolution, and Hamilton had not neglected the opportunity thus offered. While deeply engaged in the work of the Constitution, he labored at his profession, in which he had been the leader almost from his first appearance. He laid aside a lucrative practice when he took the treasury, and, having exhausted his savings while in office, returned to the bar a poor man, with his mind fixed on making money and fame as a lawyer. With his brilliant reputation as a public man and party leader, he at once received more business than he had left in 1789.

In a few months he was again at the head of the bar, and master of a large and growing practice. After the election of Jefferson he became even more absorbed in the law than before, and drifted steadily out of the current of public affairs. With this he was now well content. He said with truth that he had no desire to reënter public life, unless called forth by the contingency of a foreign or civil war. Unfortunately for himself, he considered the latter misfortune only too likely to happen.

Much might be written of Hamilton as a lawyer. His professional success has been dimmed by the brilliancy of his career as a statesman; but there can be no doubt that he deserves a very high place among those Americans who have been most distinguished at the bar. As a constitutional lawyer it is not necessary to go beyond the argument on the national bank to show a capacity in this direction of the very first order. Hamilton's powers of statement and of clear, cogent reasoning were admirably adapted for arguments to the court on points of law and equity, and in this field he shone from the outset. Fortunately, we have proof of his power before the court and also of his effectiveness with a jury, the most evanescent form of legal ability, in two very famous cases which were of sufficient importance to escape oblivion.

One was a prosecution for libel directed against Henry Croswell, the Federalist editor of a small local journal. The obnoxious paragraph was to the effect that Jefferson had paid Callender to slander Washington and Adams. This statement was not particularly outrageous, if compared to those which filled the newspapers on both sides at that time, and it had moreover already appeared in substance in the "New York Evening Post." But the Democratic leaders, now that they had come to power, were resolved to try their hand at muzzling the press and putting a stop to the stinging attacks of their opponents. They, therefore, selected a weak assailant, and prepared to make an example of him for the benefit of the Federalist editors. With a Democratic sheriff, Democratic grand jury, and Democratic judge, they obtained an indictment, after exhibiting a rough disregard of the rights of the defendant. When the case came to trial, Hamilton, who had been urged to assume the defense, was unable to appear, and the prosecution was pushed unrelentingly. Croswell's counsel asked for time, in order to get witnesses from Virginia to testify to the truth of the libel; but Judge Lewis held that the jury were judges only of the fact, and not of the truth or intent of the publication. After a night's deliberation the jury found Croswell guilty, and his counsel at once moved for a new trial on the ground of misdirection by the judge. The ruling of Judge Lewis was in direct contradiction of the famous New York precedent established in the Zenger trial, but it found support in the law of England. The issue raised the great question of general verdicts, on which Erskine won his renown and stemmed the tide of reactionary violence in London. It appealed to Hamilton both as a lawyer and statesman, and as the consistent friend of a free press in accordance with what he believed to be the true principles of the common law. He therefore laid everything aside in order to make the principal argument in support of the motion before the Supreme Court at Albany. The case excited intense interest. Every one flocked to the court room, and the legislature could not obtain a quorum. Hamilton closed the case, and the court adjourned the first day before he had finished his address. He concluded the next morning, and occupied in all six hours. His argument was a splendid piece of reasoning and eloquence, marked by all the qualities of thought and expression for which he was distinguished. Chancellor Kent, whose notes have preserved to us a description of this argument,[1] said that " it was the greatest forensic

[1] See Appendix, Note C.

effort Hamilton ever made. He had bestowed
unusual attention on the case, and he came
prepared to discuss the points of law with a
perfect mastery of the subject. There was an
unusual solemnity and earnestness on his part
in the discussion. He was, at times, highly
impassioned and pathetic. His whole soul was
enlisted in the cause. The aspect of the times
was portentous, and he was persuaded that if
he could overthrow the high-toned doctrine of
the judge it would be a great gain to the liber-
ties of this country. . . . The anxiety and tenderness of his feelings, and the gravity of his
theme, rendered his reflections exceedingly impressive. He never before in my hearing made
any effort in which he commanded higher rev-
erence for his principles, nor equal admiration
for the power and pathos of his eloquence."
There is no need to attempt any addition to this
statement. A man who could win praise, so
high and so unstinted, from such a man as
Chancellor Kent, requires no further testimony
to his rank and ability as a great lawyer.

The other famous case which has come down
to us, and to which I have already alluded, was
a murder trial, which appealed strongly to the
interest and sympathies of the community, and
which exhibited Hamilton's powers in a new
light, and one very different from that of the

prosecution of Croswell. The body of a girl
was found in a well, and her lover, a young
mechanic of good character, was suspected, in-
dicted, and put on trial for the murder. Hamilton was retained for the defense, the difficulty
of which was greatly enhanced by the strong
popular feeling against his client. The evidence was nearly all circumstantial, and Hamilton dealt with it as it was put in very effectively,
and greatly impaired its effect. The government then called their principal witness, one
Croucher, a fellow of evil repute and on whose
direct testimony the verdict depended. Hamilton had become convinced that Croucher was
the real culprit, and he knew that his evidence
was the crucial point in the case. When the
examination in chief was concluded, the night
was well advanced. Hamilton sent for two can-
dles, and by placing one on each side of the
witness box threw Croucher's face into strong
relief, and then confronted him with a fixed
and piercing gaze. Objection was made to this
procedure, but the court overruled the objection,
and Hamilton then said with deep solemnity,
" I have special reasons, deep reasons, reasons
that I dare not express, reasons that, when the
real culprit is detected and placed before the
court, will then be understood." He paused,
and the attention of every one was riveted in

breathless silence upon the witness. Hamilton continued: "The jury will mark every muscle of his face, every motion of his eye. I conjure you to look through that man's countenance to his conscience." A severe cross-examination followed. The wretched witness stumbled, contradicted himself, and utterly broke down. The jury acquitted the prisoner without leaving their seats. The subsequent history of Croucher,[1] who left the court room covered with suspicion and contumely, justified Hamilton's device, which under ordinary circumstances would not be permissible. The incident shows in Hamilton that quickness of apprehension, force of personality, and fertility of resource as well as the dramatic sense, which are all such important and necessary qualities to great advocates before a jury. These two cases, in different ways, are good illustrations of Hamilton's power and success at the bar.

The popular belief in the certainty of Hamilton's winning cases was extraordinary, and while it brought him briefs without number it reveals at the same time the great secret of his success as an advocate. Men came to think that, if he ex-

---

[1] Croucher was convicted of rape on a child, was pardoned, went to Virginia, there committed a fraud, and fled to England, where he is said to have been executed for a heinous crime.

rted himself, he could compel any one, whether judge or juryman, to agree with him. This idea sprang from a vague perception of what was, in reality, the very essence of Hamilton's mind and character. Force of intellect and force of will were the sources of his success. Eloquence he had in abundance, but it was that of the parliamentary orator and debater rather than that of the advocate to a jury. He was, above all things, fitted for the Senate, and it was the eloquence of the Senate that he brought into the courts. He rarely attempted to deal with that complicated machine, a jury, by any of the various and difficult methods characteristic of the greatest advocates; but he addressed them as he did a convention, or as he did the public when he spoke through his essays, always relying, mainly, on his power to carry conviction to their reason. Yet he never forgot, when he was speaking, that while he convinced he must also persuade, that reason must not only be satisfied, but prejudices subdued. He supported arguments by resorting to the emotions. He was full of pathos, fervor, and indignation, and when he was stirred they gave warmth and light to all he said. He never indulged in rhetorical flourishes, and his style was simple and severe. He seldom sought to move the passions of men through their imagination. Directness was his

most distinguishing characteristic, and whether
he appealed to the head or the heart, he went
straight to the mark. The secret lay in the
force with which he did it. It was the passionate energy, the strong nature, the commanding,
irresistible will, which carried his hearers by
storm when reasoning had made a practicable
breach, and these were the qualities which made
men believe that Hamilton could extort assent
and compel submission from the most stubborn
and unwilling opponent.

But while Hamilton was thus employed in
winning fortune and in adding the fame of the
great lawyer to that of the distinguished statesman, while he was ever withdrawing more and
more from politics, planning a great work on
civil government, enjoying his family and or-
dering the affairs of his farm, at that moment
his fate was close upon him. He continued, of
course, to take an interest and a more or less
active part in public concerns. The Federalists
broke up rapidly after their defeat, but he was
still the trusted chief of all who held together.
Whenever the responsibility of leadership forced
him to act he never shrank from the duty, and
it was one of these occasions that brought him
to his death.

Aaron Burr defeated Hamilton in the struggle for the control of New York, which cost the

Federalists the presidency, but he could not drive his great opponent from his path. Hamilton had stood between him and a foreign mission, and came again athwart his course by frustrating his intrigue for the presidency. Thus baffled among the Federalists, Burr turned to his own party only to see his power waning, and to encounter the dislike and suspicion of Jefferson. The crafty Virginian was bent on the destruction of his would-be rival, and Burr soon found himself hopelessly entangled in the subtilely woven meshes of presidential intrigues, and falling helplessly toward certain ruin. To extricate himself from the disastrous field of national politics, he sought the governorship of New York, behind which was the possibility of a northern confederacy and presidency, — a phantom evoked by the murmurs of secession now heard among New England leaders. Again Hamilton arose and stood in the way of these intrigues, denouncing the schemes of secession, and so dividing the Federalists of New York as to give the election to Lewis, Burr's Democratic rival. Then it was that Burr determined upon revenge. Vengeance must have been his principal if not his only motive, inasmuch as killing Hamilton was not likely to improve his own condition, even though it removed his arch enemy. In 1800 there were many stronger incentives to call Hamilton out than in 1804, but Burr had then held his peace and bided his time. Now, however, his political fortunes were desperate, and the obloquy sure to come upon him if Hamilton fell by his hand could hardly make matters worse. With cool deliberation he set about forcing a quarrel. He showed his purpose plainly enough by selecting a remark attributed to Hamilton at the time of the caucuses held to nominate candidates for the governorship, which was really applicable to his general public character, was not peculiarly severe, and was perfectly inoffensive, compared with many of the denunciations launched at him by Hamilton only a few years before. Hamilton had no desire to fight, but it was impossible to avoid it, if he admitted the force of the code of honor, when Burr was determined to fix a quarrel upon him. There was an exchange of letters, and finally a meeting was arranged.

Aaron Burr, who was now on the eve of committing the deed which has done more than anything else in his worthless life to keep his memory alive, belonged to a not uncommon variety of the human species. He was one of the conspirator class of which Napoleon III. furnished the most conspicuous example in modern times. It has been the fashion to portray Burr as a being of great but misguided intellect, a human Mephistopheles, — grand, evil, mysterious. In reality he was a shallow man, with a superficial brilliancy, and the conspirator's talent for intrigue of all sorts. He was a successful rake, — bad, unscrupulous, tricky, possessing what women and young men call "fascination," and utterly devoid of any moral sense. He would not stab or poison Hamilton, for he was not a common villain, and had a due respect for criminal and social law. But he was perfectly ready to call Hamilton out and kill him if he could under the rules of a recognized code. This duel has been often spoken of as a murder. In the forum of conscience, before the tribunal of moral laws, Burr was no doubt a murderer ; but by the code which he and Hamilton alike recognized, and by the system under which they were brought up, Burr acted in strict accordance with his rights. Hamilton certainly had no ground to complain. He was a fighting man, and he had always admitted the force of the duelist's code of honor. Over and over again he had described Burr in language which, as he was well aware, implied in that day a readiness to answer for it in the field. The fact that on this occasion the words might be confined strictly to Burr's public character availed nothing. Hamilton had repeatedly used "fighting words" in speaking of Burr, and the latter had the right to demand a reckoning for any particular sentence he might select. There seems to be little doubt that Burr had come to Hamilton not long before in great pecuniary distress, and had been relieved with that large-hearted generosity in which Hamilton never failed. This incident casts a still deeper shade of infamy upon Burr's blackened character, but it does not affect his standing under the code. The code of honor, so called, was bad and false, barbarous even, but those who lived by it were responsible to it and for it. When Hamilton attacked Burr as he did, he ran the risk of a challenge which he could accept or decline as he chose. Such a challenge did not, according to the code of honor, make Burr a murderer, nor did he become one by practicing at a mark before fighting. Every Frenchman, if he has time, goes to the Salle d'Armes before fighting, and a man has as much right to prepare for a duel as for a boat-race or a boxing match. The pity of it all is, that Hamilton felt obliged to yield assent to the requirements of the code.

Each man prepared for the meeting in his own fashion; Burr by pistol practice in his garden, Hamilton by settling the business of his clients. As the fatal day drew near, Hamilton displayed a calm cheerfulness, such as became a gallant man of strong character, and wrote

farewell letters to his wife full of the most intense feeling and touching pathos. Burr took
the necessary precautions for the destruction of
compromising letters from women whom he had
seduced. They met at last, on a beautiful July
morning, by the banks of the Hudson. Hamilton fell at the first fire, mortally wounded, dis-
charging his own pistol into the air. He was
taken to his home, lingered a few hours in terrible pain, and died, surrounded by his agonized
family. Burr went forth unharmed, to engage
in abortive treason, and to become a wanderer
and an outcast on the face of the earth.

Hamilton's suffering and death caused an
outburst of bitter and indignant grief among
men of all parties throughout the nation, which
has been equaled only in our own time by the
popular emotion at the murders of Lincoln and
Garfield. The people knew that a great man
had fallen. The senseless slaughter of a famous
statesman, the useless, needless sacrifice of a
man of brilliant abilities in the prime of life,
was felt to be almost as much a disgrace as a
misfortune, and Hamilton's death did more to
abate dueling and make it odious than any
event in our history.

The question, however, which presses on us
as we consider the circumstances of Hamilton's
death is, why did he fight? why did such a man

as he bow before the code to which he fell a victim? It was something far deeper than mere
loyalty to a system which he, like other men of
his stamp, had accepted as they found it. Hamilton could have set his foot upon the code. The
personal courage of the man who stormed the
Yorktown redoubt was beyond question or cavil.
He could have said : " I renounce the code ; it is
senseless and barbarous. I have attacked you
as a public•man, and I choose to consider· it a
purely public matter. I decline to fight." He
could have said this, and he would have said it
had he not felt that the need of conforming to
certain prejudices made the sacrifice imperative.
Before he went to the fatal meeting he put upon
paper a statement which gave with his own
unrivaled force and clearness the objections to
dueling, and the seemingly all-powerful motives
which urged him to refuse to risk his life and
the welfare of his children. At the end of this
remarkable paper he gives his reason for meeting Burr in these words: " The ability to be
in future useful, whether in resisting mischief
or effecting good, in those crises of our public affairs which seem likely to happen, would
probably be inseparable from a conformity with
public prejudice in this particular." Hamilton
was a man, not only of courage enough to fight
a duel, but he possessed that far higher courage

which would have enabled him to refuse the challenge and face a public prejudice, the strength of which in his own case he sadly overestimated. What, then, were the possible crises which he foresaw, and which led to his fatal decision?

The opinions which caused these apprehensions are of the utmost importance to a correct understanding of his life and work. They furnish the key to the principles which guided him through a large part of his career as a public man, and they produced certain settled beliefs which finally drove him to accept Burr's challenge and thus hurried him to his death. I propose, therefore, to trace the growth and development of these opinions by means of extracts from his letters. In these passages we shall see the effect upon Hamilton of the French Revolution, and the dangers which he came to believe threatened the country. We shall then understand the nature of the crisis which haunted his imagination, and which caused him to sacrifice his life. In these same passages we shall also learn incidentally, from his own lips, how intense was his love of nationality and how deep his hatred of secession; and we shall see, too, in the most striking way, how purely national were the principles which inspired his foreign policy, and how utterly baseless were the accusations of undue sympathy with Great Britain.

The first extract is from a letter to Lafayette written in October, 1789, when everything
looked so fair and smiling at the dawn of the
French Revolution. We see here the remarkable penetration and statesmanlike prescience
of Hamilton, as well as his knowledge and keen
perception of forces, social and political, as he
points out the dangers which he dreaded and
which hardly any one then foresaw, but which
all came to pass. In his fears we detect, too,
the first germs of his subsequent opinions. He
says to his old comrade-in-arms : —

"I have seen with a mixture of pleasure and apprehension the progress of the events which have
lately taken place in your country. As a friend to
mankind and to liberty I rejoice in the efforts you are
making to establish it, while I fear much for the final
success of the attempts, for the fate of those I esteem
who are engaged in it, and for the danger, in case of
success, of innovations greater than will consist with
the real felicity of your nation. If your affairs still
go well, when this reaches you, you will ask why this
foreboding of ill, when all the appearances have been
so much in your favor. I will tell you : I dread dis-
agreements among those who are now united (which
will be likely to be improved by the adverse party),
about the nature of your constitution. I dread the
vehement character of your people, whom I fear you
may find it more easy to bring on, than to keep
within proper bounds after you have put them in

motion. I dread the interested refractoriness of your
nobles who cannot all be gratified, and who may be
unwilling to submit to the requisite sacrifices. And
I dread the reveries of your philosophic politicians,
who appear in the movement to have great influence,
and who, being mere speculatists, may aim at more
refinement than suits either with human nature or
the composition of your nation."

The next extract is from a letter written
rather more than three years later, when these
early anticipations had become terrible realities,
and when the storms of the revolution had begun to disturb our own politics. Speculation
as to results in France was at an end. All the
possibilities that Hamilton had dreaded then
were accomplished facts, and he was now anxious to know how much the same perils were
to be feared in this country. He wrote to his
friend Colonel Carrington, in April, 1793, to
learn the state of public opinion in Virginia;
and from Carrington's reply we discover what
his inquiries were, and thus catch the drift of
his thought at that time. He wished to know
what the feeling was in Virginia as to the revolutionary cause in France; as to the execution
of the king, the adoption of a neutrality policy
by the United States, the maintenance or aban-
donment of the French treaties, and as to the
reception of Genet. He soon felt assured, ap-

parently, that the same dangerous forces existed
in this country as in France, and only doubted as
to their extent and power among the people. In
a letter of the same year (1793), after describing with marked disgust Genet's reception on
arriving in Philadelphia, he speaks of the promoters of the affair as the opponents of the government and disturbers of order, and then says:

" We too have our disorganizers. But I trust
there is enough of virtue and good sense in the people of America to baffle every attempt against their
prosperity, though masked under the specious garb of
an extraordinary zeal for liberty. They practically,
I doubt not, adopt this sacred maxim, that without
government there is no true liberty."

Having already expressed his belief in the
probability of " combinations " to control our
politics in foreign interests, he then goes on
after the passage just quoted to deprecate violent demonstrations of attachment to France,
and to repudiate all comparisons between her
revolution and ours. " I own I do not like the
comparison," he says, and then follow his reasons, which are worth giving in full because
they state in a moderate and yet forcible manner the grounds for his opinions as to the dominant movement of the age, and express very
admirably the causes and the reasoning on which
his principles and those of the Federalists gen-

erally were founded. It is an excellent exposition of the feelings which actuated the opposition to the French Revolution and its theories: —

" When I contemplate the horrid and systematic massacres of the 2d and 3d of September; when I observe that a Marat and a Robespierre, the notorious promoters of these bloody scenes, sit triumphantly in the convention and take a conspicuous part in its measures, that an attempt to bring the assassins to justice has been obliged to be abandoned; when I see an unfortunate prince, whose reign was a continued demonstration of the goodness and benevolence of his heart, of his attachment to the people of whom he was the monarch, who though educated in the lap of despotism, had given repeated proofs that he was not the enemy of liberty, brought precipitately and ignominiously to the block without any substantial proof of guilt as yet disclosed, — without even an authentic exhibition of motives, in decent regard to the opinions of mankind; when I find the doctrines of atheism openly advanced in the convention and heard with loud applause; when I see the sword of fanaticism extended to force a political creed upon citizens who were invited to submit to the arms of France as the harbingers of liberty; when I behold the hand of rapacity outstretched to prostrate and ravish the monuments of religious worship erected by those citizens and their ancestors; when I perceive passion, tumult, and violence usurping those seats where reason and cool deliberation ought to prevail, I acknowledge that

I am glad to believe there is no real resemblance between what was the cause of America and what is
the cause of France; that the difference is no less
great than that between liberty and licentiousness. I
regret whatever has a tendency to compound them,
and I feel anxious, as an American, that the ebullitions of inconsiderate men among us may not tend to
involve our reputation in the issue."

Two years later he felt that there was danger
of actual outbreaks at a time when our relations
with France had become very strained and threatening. The dangerous elements, he seems to
have thought, were really on the verge of open
violence in New York. He writes to Wolcott
in July, 1795 : —

"We have some cause to suspect, though not
enough to believe, that our Jacobins meditate serious
mischief to certain individuals. It happens that the
militia of this city, from the complexion of its officers,
cannot in general be depended on, and it will be difficult for some time to organize a competent armed
substitute. In this situation our eyes turn as a resource in a sudden emergency, upon the military
now in the forts, but these, we are told, are under
marching orders. Pray converse confidentially with
the secretary at war and engage him to suspend the
march. Matters in eight or ten days will explain
themselves."

The next extract gives a glimpse of Hamilton's theory of foreign policy, and of the purely

national spirit which inspired it. The last
clause shows how deeply he felt the evil of the
colonial mode of thought, which was then so
strong that men did not even realize that they
were still beneath its influence. Hamilton already anticipated the essential need of that
intellectual freedom and individuality toward
Europe which it took years of conflict to bring
to pass. The letter is dated December 16, 1796,
and is addressed to Rufus King : —

"The favorable change in the conduct of Great
Britain towards us, strengthens the hands of the
friends of order and peace. It is much to be desired
that a treatment in all respects unexceptionable from
that quarter should obviate all pretext to inflame the
public mind.

"We are laboring hard to establish in this country principles more and more *national*, and free from
all foreign ingredients, so that we may be neither
'Greeks nor Trojans,' but truly Americans."

A few months later (April 10, 1797) he shows
strongly in a letter to William Smith how averse
he was to violence, either in favor of or against
any foreign people whatsoever, whether they
were the English, whom he respected, or the
French, whom he detested, because he knew that
such violence was inconsistent, not only with dignity, but with a true national pride : —

"It is unpleasant to me to know that I have for some time differed materially from many of my friends on public subjects, and I particularly regret, that at the present critical juncture there is in my apprehension much danger that *sensibility* will be an overmatch for policy. We seem now to feel and reason as the *Jacobins* did when Great Britain insulted and injured us, though certainly we have at least as much need of a temperate conduct now as we had then. I only say God grant that the public interest may not be sacrificed at the shrine of irritation and mistaken pride."

The same feeling finds expression in the following passage from a letter to Oliver Wolcott, dated June 6, 1797 : —

"I like very well the course of executive conduct in regard to the controversy with France, and I like the answer of the Senate in regard to the President's speech.

"But I confess, I have not been well satisfied with the answer reported in the House. It contains too many hard expressions; and hard words are very rarely used in public proceedings. Mr. Jay and other friends here have been struck in the same manner with myself. We shall not regret to see the answer softened down. *Real firmness* is good for everything. *Strut* is good for nothing."

In a similar strain he writes to Pickering a few months later (March 27, 1798), defining the proper relations to be maintained with England, in case the war against France should be actively prosecuted : —

"I am against going immediately into alliance with Great Britain. It is my opinion that her interests will insure us her coöperation to the extent of her power, and that a treaty will not secure her further. On the other hand a treaty might entangle us. Public opinion is not prepared for it."

England, he says, should give sufficient powers to her minister here to meet all exigencies, and to enter into alliance if opportunity and public opinion permitted it. Then he refers to the necessity of acquiring Louisiana, which at that moment held a leading place in his thoughts.

In the next letter, which I shall quote, we see, for the first time, a plain allusion to the "crisis" which might in the event of its occurrence have a decisive effect upon his actions and upon his career. The letter is addressed to Jay, who wished to appoint Hamilton to the vacancy in the United States Senate caused by the resignation of Judge Hobart, and is dated April 24, 1798.

"I have received your two favors of the 19th instant. I feel, as I ought, the mark of confidence they announce. But I am obliged by my situation to decline the appointment. This situation you are too well acquainted with to render it necessary for me to

enter into explanation. There may arrive a crisis
when I may conceive myself bound once more to sacrifice the interests of my family to public call. But
I must defer the change as long as possible."

How deeply rooted his convictions had now
become as to the dangers to be apprehended
from the influence of France and of French
ideas, and how real and menacing he felt these
perils to be in the United States, are well illustrated in a letter to Washington, dated May 19,
1798. I have already referred to this letter in
a previous chapter, but the passage in question
deserves a full quotation in this connection.

"It is more and more evident that the powerful
faction which has for years opposed the government,
is determined to go every length with France. I am
sincere in declaring my full conviction, as the result
of a long course of observation, that they are ready
to *new model* our constitution under the *influence*
or *coercion* of France; to form with her a perpetual
alliance, *offensive* and *defensive*, and to give her a
monopoly of our trade by *peculiar* and *exclusive* priv-
ileges. This would be in substance, whatever it
might be in name, to make this country a province
of France. Neither do I doubt that her standard,
displayed in this country, would be directly or indi-
rectly seconded by them, in pursuance of the project
I have mentioned."

His fears of social confusion were not only,

as we see here, fully aroused, but his pride in American nationality was deeply touched. In another passage, in the same letter, his dread and dislike of anything sectional in our politics, or of anything suggesting geographical division, and consequent secession, come out very strikingly.

"It is painful and alarming to remark that the opposition faction assumes so much a geographical complexion. As yet, from the south of Maryland, nothing has been heard, but accounts of disapprobation of our government, and approbation of or apology for France. This is a most portentous symptom and demands every human effort to change it."

The mischiefs which he anticipated seemed to him in this exciting year to be so close at hand that we find him preparing in his own mind practical measures for meeting and overcoming them. His first thought, of course, was for the army, upon which he relied for the maintenance of order and government. It was with this purpose that he wrote as follows to Otis, December 27, 1798 : —

"Any reduction of the actual force appears to me inexpedient. It will argue to our enemies that we are either very narrow in our resources, or that our jealousy of his designs has abated. Besides, that with a view to the possibility of internal disorders alone, the force authorized is not too considerable.

The efficacy of militia for suppressing such disorders
is not too much to be relied on."

The army was his chief reliance, but he also
had an extended plan for the proper course to
be pursued by the Federalists now that they
were in possession of all branches of the government. This policy is fully set forth in the
well-known letter to Dayton, written in 1799.
I have already referred to it and given an
outline of its contents. It advised a vigorous
strengthening of the central government in all
directions, including a division of the large
States, and the enactment of sharp alien and
sedition laws. It is, as I have said, the best
exposition of Hamilton's views at that trying
period, is strongly characteristic of its author,
and was so far as possible carried out by the
Federalists.

A little later in the same year, and in a similar spirit, he wrote to ask the attorney-general,
Hoffman, to prosecute a newspaper which had
charged him with suppressing the " ' Aurora ' by
pecuniary means."

" Hitherto," he says, " I have forborne to resort to
the laws for the punishment of the authors or abettors
(of such attacks), and were I to consult personal con-
siderations alone, I should continue in this course,
repaying hatred with contempt. But public motives
now compel me to a different conduct. The designs

of that faction to overturn our government, and with
it the great pillars of social security and happiness in
this country, become every day more manifest, and
have of late acquired a system which renders them
formidable."

He then adds that one engine for the destruction of society is the issue of libels calculated
to destroy the character of the most conspicuous supporters of the government, as in this instance, by charging them with attempts to stifle
the liberty of the press ; and he says that these
intrigues and calumnies are carried on by American citizens aided by foreign gold.

The immediate danger which Hamilton
dreaded at the time of the troubles with France
dropped out of sight during the heated struggles
which preceded the election of 1800. Peace
came, too, bringing quiet in its train everywhere, and, while it served to make the conta-
gion of French principles appear less virulent,
it also pushed the "crisis," which Hamilton
always anticipated, still farther into the background. After the excitement of the political
battle had subsided, and when nothing was left
but to watch the course of the Democratic party
in full possession of the government, Hamilton
seems to have given way to a depression in regard to public affairs very unusual to his strong
nature. It seemed to him that all his labors

had been wasted and misunderstood, and that his achievements, and those of the great party which he had led, would crumble away beneath the gradual assaults of the now triumphant opposition. In this mood he wrote bitterly to Gouverneur Morris, giving vent to the disappointment which filled his soul when he thought of the success of his enemies, the seeming ingratitude of the people, and, as he believed, the waste and misapprehension of all the efforts which he had made for the welfare and glory of his country. The letter in question is dated February 27, 1802 : —

"Mine is an odd destiny," he says. "Perhaps no man in the United States has sacrificed or done more for the present Constitution than myself ; and, contrary to all my anticipations of its fate, as you know, from the very beginning. I am still laboring to prop the frail and worthless fabric. Yet I have the murmurs of its friends no less than the curses of its foes for my reward. What can I do better than withdraw from the scene? Every day proves to me more and more that this American world was not made for me.

"The time may ere long arrive when the minds of men will be prepared to make an effort to *recover* the Constitution, but the many cannot now be brought to make a stand for its preservation. We must wait a while.

"You, friend Morris, are by birth a native of this country, but by *genius* an exotic. You mistake if

premacy.   Then would the country be menaced
with anarchy and ruin; property would be con-
fiscated, society broken up, religion trampled
under foot, and everything that makes life worth
having would be in jeopardy.   Then the salvation of the country and the preservation of constitutional liberty would demand a party of
order, an army, and a leader ready to play the
part of a savior of society, and establish the
government on strong and enduring foundations.   That great part, Hamilton felt, would
fall to him, and if the contingency had been
possible, there can be no doubt that he was the
man to whom the party of order would have
turned.   He could not do this, he could not
stand at the head of an army, if it were possible
for any man to cast even the most groundless
imputation upon his personal courage.   He was
utterly at fault in supposing that there were in
the United States the same elements and the
same forces as in France.   Both race and history made their existence impossible.   The representative democracy developing in America
was more hostile to the anarchy of the French
Revolution than the strongest and most energetic
government which the wit of man could devise.
Hamilton's mistake was neither unnatural nor
uncommon; but, joined with his just belief of
the duty which would devolve upon him in such

a crisis as he anticipated, it made it imperative
for him to accept the challenge of Burr. It is
neither fanciful nor strained to regard Hamilton's death as a result of the opinions bred by
the French Revolution. That terrible convul-
sion had many illustrious victims of all nations
and all creeds, but hardly one more brilliant or
more uselessly sacrificed than the great statesman who fell before Burr's pistol that peaceful
July morning.

Thus far I have dealt with Hamilton solely
as a public man. It is, indeed, difficult to approach him in any other way, when his life and
talents were given so constantly and so completely to the service of the public. He died a
private man, mourned by a nation; he had lived,
except in his very last years, immersed in the
affairs of the commonwealth and in the full
glare of publicity. Every act of his was scrutinized and examined, every slip chronicled, every
mistake magnified, while he stood for years in
the highest places, assuming every responsibility
and conspicuous before the eyes of all men.
This unsparing publicity, which pursued Hamilton in his life, has attended him in his death.
No American, except Washington, has had
everything which he ever wrote, said, or did,
published with such elaboration as has fallen to

the lot of Hamilton. No other American has been, historically speaking, so much discussed, so much criticised, and so much written about. All this enhances the difficulty of any fresh study of Hamilton's life; but at the same time, even the briefest biography would be incomplete without an attempt, at least, to portray him as a man, to analyze the traits of his mind and character, and to define the quality of his greatness.

In person Hamilton was well made, of light and active build, but very small, much below the average height. His friends were wont to call him the "little lion;" and it is somewhat remarkable that his stature seems to have interfered so slightly, if at all, with his success as an orator. A commanding and imposing presence is a great aid in affecting an audience, and yet Hamilton was one of the most impressive speakers of his time. He was, too, the most eloquent man and the most effective advocate of his day, whether in court or in convention, if we can judge by results, by the fragments that remain of his speeches, and by the testimony of eye-witnesses. There was certainly no one who was in active public life during the same period, unless it be John Adams, or Fisher Ames on one memorable occasion, who could for a moment be compared with him as an orator. It is very plain, too, that Hamilton's success in this direc-

tion was by no means wholly due to what he
said, or to his power of reasoning and of lucid
and forcible statement. The man was impressive. Inches of stature and of girth were lack-
ing, but he was none the less full of dignity. In
this, of course, his looks helped him. His head
was finely shaped, symmetrical, and massive.
His eyes were dark, deep-set, and full of light
and fire. He had a long, rather sharp nose, a
well-shaped, close-set mouth, and a strong, firm
jaw. The characteristics of the spare, clean-cut
features are penetration and force. There is a
piercing look about the face even in repose; and
when Hamilton was moved a fire came into his
eyes which we are told had a marvelous effect.
But it was the soul which shone through his
eyes, and animated his mobile countenance, that
made him so effective in speech. As men listened to him, they felt profoundly the mastery of
the strong nature, the imperious will, and the
passionate energy which gave such force to his
pathos, to his invective, and to the even flow of
clear, telling argument. The impression which
Hamilton was capable of producing is well illustrated by the famous scene of the murder trial,
when he laid bare the guilt of Croucher. Yet
the excitement of a court-room was not necessary to such a feat. In the quiet of an office,
solely by his own resistless determination he

wrested a conveyance, which was unjust and had been unfairly obtained, from the oppressor of his client.

In private life Hamilton was much beloved and most attractive. He talked well and freely. He was open-hearted and hospitable, full of high spirits and geniality. In his own family he was idolized by wife and children. The affection which he inspired in all who knew him was largely due to the perfect generosity of his nature, for he gave time and money with a lavish hand to all who sought his aid. He carried this habit into his business to his own detriment. He would often refuse to make any charge to poor clients, and never could be persuaded to accept anything beyond a reasonable and modest fee. He had in truth a contempt for money, and, while he made a nation's fortune, he never made his own. At his death he left his family little except his name and fame.

Like most men of great talents and strong will, Hamilton had a large measure of self-confidence. Just after he left the treasury, he feared that Congress would fail to treat the finances in a proper way. He wrote to a friend in great wrath that he would not stand tamely by and see the nation disgraced; if Congress did not do their duty they would have to reckon with him. On another occasion he was dis-

pleased by what he considered a useless demand
for information on the part of the Senate. He
thereupon addressed a communication[1] to that
august body in which he lectured them as to
their conduct, and took them to task roundly
for their misbehavior. This letter is quite a
curiosity, and the meekness with which the
Senate apparently accepted the rebuke is not
the least amusing part of the affair. All this
was thoroughly characteristic of the man. The
greater the odds the more defiantly and the
more confidently he faced opposition. On one
or two occasions this self-confidence took the
more disagreeable form of self-assertion, but
such outbreaks were rare.

Hamilton's defects sprang not from weakness
but from the strength of his passions, which
sometimes overmastered his reason. Thus it was
in his relations with women, which had an un-
enviable notoriety. It was passion again which
led him into the unworthy proposition to Governor Jay and into his wild attack upon Adams.
His faults were those of a powerful and passionate nature when it had broken down all the
barriers of self-control. His errors are all the
more to be regretted because he was a man of

[1] The letter is given in full in Adams's *Life of Gallatin*, p.
116, and is also to be found in *American State Papers ; Claims*,
p. 77.

such wide influence and striking abilities, and for this reason they were, of course, all the more dangerous.

There is no better evidence of Hamilton's greatness than is to be found in the letters and sayings of his bitterest enemies. Burr pronounced the man to be lost who put himself on paper with him. Jefferson called him the " Colossus of the Federalists," and always referred to the acts and opinions of his opponents as those of Hamilton, speaking of that party by the name of its leader. Ambrose Spencer, the distinguished judge, who had had many conflicts with Hamilton, and, on at least one occasion, had felt the edge of his sarcasm, paid him one of the handsomest tributes ever rendered to his abilities, at the same time characterizing the quality of his greatness and his influence with peculiar felicity : —

" Alexander Hamilton," said Spencer, " was the greatest man this country ever produced. I knew him well. I was in situations often to observe and study him. I saw him at the bar and at home. He argued cases before me while I sat as judge on the bench. Webster has done the same. In power of reasoning Hamilton was the equal of Webster ; and more than this can be said of no man. In creative power Hamilton was infinitely Webster's superior. . . . It was he, more than any other man, who

thought out the Constitution of the United States and
the details of the government of the Union; and, out
of the chaos that existed after the Revolution, raised
a fabric every part of which is instinct with his
thought. I can truly say that hundreds of politicians and statesmen of the day get both the web and
woof of their thoughts from Hamilton's brains. He,
more than any man, did the thinking of the time."

Chancellor Kent, who was one of Hamilton's
warmest admirers, says of him that —

"He rose at once to the loftiest heights of professional eminence, by his profound penetration, his
power of analysis, the comprehensive grasp and
strength of his understanding, and the firmness,
frankness, and integrity of his character. We may
say of him, in reference to his associates, as was said
of Papinian: 'Omnes longo post se intervallo re-
liquerit.' "

There is not much to choose between the
praise of the quondam foe and of the constant
friend. Both the Federalist and the Democrat,
eminent lawyers and judges both, were agreed
as to Hamilton's ability.

Among the Federalists Hamilton had a band
of devoted friends who comprised a very large
proportion of the most distinguished men in the
nation. They were an able, strong, hard-headed,
and rather dogmatic body, most of them leaders themselves, and holding high places in the

republic. Yet they supported Hamilton with
a fidelity which has been rarely equaled. The
roll of his followers is enough by itself to establish his position in American history. Indifference was impossible toward Hamilton. He was
too strong and too open to inspire lukewarm
sentiments, and he was loved and hated with
equal intensity. At the same time Hamilton,
as I have already said, was preëminently a
leader of leaders. He could do " the thinking
of his time; " he could issue orders, or plan a
policy, or act in conjunction with men who followed or sustained him in obedience to the dic-
tates of reason. But he was never an adept in
the difficult and delicate art of managing men
wherein his great rival Jefferson stood supreme.
He was as far as possible from being a demagogue, and he was not even a popular leader,
for he had too great a distrust of democracy
to appeal successfully to the sympathy of the
masses. In this he was a fit and typical leader
of the party to which he belonged. He could
not float with the currents of public sentiment
and had no faith in them. He was a leader,
and could not follow. He could mark out a
path and walk in it, and, if the people hesitated
or held back, he would walk alone. This did
not arise from narrowness, for Hamilton had
always great liberality of mind, but simply from

the strength of his convictions and from reliance
on his own abilities, which made it impossible
for him to seek for success by yielding a jot of
what he believed, after mature deliberation, to
be right and true. This implies, of course,
great force of character; but Hamilton had also
a boldness of disposition which stamped itself
on his financial and foreign policy, and at times
amounted to an almost reckless audacity. The
miserable Reynolds affair has cast a shadow upon
the honor of James Monroe, and its wretched
details have found a place in one of the biogra-
phies of Jefferson. No one can desire to rake
over the ashes of this miserable scandal, but in
its effect it showed the courage of Hamilton in
a most striking manner. Drawn by his un-
curbed passion into a low intrigue with a worthless woman, he found himself threatened with a
black imputation upon his official integrity. At
the cost of bitter grief to himself and to all
whom he most loved, he published a pamphlet
in which he told the whole unpleasant story.
The manliness of the act, the self-inflicted punishment, and the high sense of public honor
thus exhibited, silenced even his opponents; but
the confession was one which must have wrung
Hamilton to the quick, and it shows an amount
of nerve and determination for which our history can furnish no parallel.

Hamilton's career as a public man had closed before his death. Had he lived longer he would have added to his reputation as a lawyer and writer ; but it is very doubtful if he would have again entered public life. His work was done. It was a great work, and had been well performed. He cared but little for office. He was ambitious, but his objects were fame and power, to be obtained by advancing the welfare and dignity of his country. So long as he could lead his party and help to shape the national policy, he was perfectly content to remain in a lawyer's chambers in New York. A great office had to him no value in itself, but only in what he was able to achieve by holding it; and every one will admit that few men have accomplished so much. He founded the financial system of the United States, and converted the barren clauses of the Constitution into a living organism. He established the doctrine of a liberal construction and of the implied powers; and he shares with Washington the honor of devising and carrying out the foreign policy of the United States. This is enough. There is no need to rehearse the almost endless list of lesser matters which bear the mark of his fertile and powerful intellect. He was always at work, and we look in vain for sterile places in his life.

There are two classes of statesmen, — those

who are great in their calling, and those who, in addition, represent great ideas. Instances of the former kind abound. Examples of the latter are rare. Hamilton is one of the statesmen of creative minds who represent great ideas. It is for this reason that he left the deep mark of his personal influence upon our history. His principles of finance, of foreign affairs, of political economy, and of the powers and duties of government under the Constitution, may be found on every page of our history, and are full of vitality to-day. But Hamilton is identified with two other ideas which go far deeper, and which have been the moving forces in our national development. He did not believe in democracy as a system of government. He strove with all his energy to make the experiment of the Constitution succeed, but he doubted its merit at the outset, and finally came to the conclusion that in its existing form it was doomed to failure. He believed in class influence and representation, in strong government, and in what, for want of a better phrase, may be called an aristocratic republic. Curiously enough, this theory was put in practice only in the South, where Hamilton had scarcely any followers.

The other great idea of which he was the embodiment was that of nationality. No other man of that period, except Washington, was

fully imbued with the national spirit. To Hamilton it was the very breath of his public life,
the essence of his policy. To this grand principle many men, especially in later times, have
rendered splendid services and made noble sacrifices; but there is no single man to whom it
owes more than to Hamilton. In a time when
American nationality meant nothing, he grasped
the great conception in all its fullness, and gave
all he had of will and intellect to make its real-
ization possible. He and Washington alone perceived the destiny which was in store for the
republic. For this he declared that the United
States must aim at an ascendant in the affairs
of America. For this he planned the conquest
of Louisiana and the Floridas, and, despite the
frowns of his friends, rose above all party feelings and sustained Jefferson in his unhesitating
seizure of the opportunity to acquire that vast
territory by purchase. To these ends everything
he did was directed, and in his task of founding
a government he also founded a nation. It was
a great work. Others contributed much to it,
but Hamilton alone fully understood it. On the
other side was Jefferson, also a man who represented ideas, that of democracy and that of a
confederacy, with a weak general government
and powerful states threatening secession. The
ideas which these two men embodied have in

their conflict made up the history of the United
States. The democratic principles of Jefferson
and the national principles of Hamilton have
prevailed, and have sway to-day throughout the
length and breadth of the land. But, if we go
a step farther, we find that the great Federalist
has the advantage. The democratic system of
Jefferson is administered in the form and on the
principles of Hamilton; and while the former
went with the current and fell in with the dominant forces of the time, Hamilton established
his now accepted principles, and carried his projects to completion in the face of a relentless
opposition, and against the mistaken wishes of a
large part of the people.

To attempt to measure the exact proportions
of a great man is neither very easy nor perhaps
very profitable. This biography has been written to little purpose if it has failed to show the
influence of Hamilton upon our history, and this
of itself is a title of the highest distinction. It
is given to but few men to impress themselves
indelibly upon the history of a great nation.
But Hamilton, as a man, achieved even more
than this. His versatility was extraordinary.
He was a great orator and lawyer, and he was
also the ablest political and constitutional writer
of his day, a good soldier, and possessed of a
wonderful capacity for organization and prac-

tical administration.   He was a master in every
field that he entered, and however he may have
erred in moments of passion, he never failed.
Weakness and incompetency were not to be
found in Hamilton.   Comparisons are valueless,
because points of difference between men are
endless.   John Marshall ranked Hamilton next
to Washington, and with the judgment of their
great chief justice Americans are wont to be
content.   But wherever he is placed, so long as
the people of the United States form one nation,
the name of Alexander Hamilton will be held in
high and lasting honor, and even in the wreck
of governments that noble intellect would still
command the homage of men.

APPENDIX

NOTE A.

MR. BANCROFT in the eighth volume of his history of the United States (page 79), in describing the great meeting at New York in July, 1774, says: "It has been kept in memory, that on this occasion a young man from abroad, so small and delicate in his organization that he appeared to be much younger than perhaps he really was, took part in the debate before the crowd. . . . He proved to be Alexander Hamilton, a West Indian. His mother, while he was yet a child, had left him an orphan and poor. A father's care he seems never to have known. The first written trace of his existence is in 1766, when his name appears as witness to a legal paper executed in the Danish island of Santa Cruz." I have followed in my first chapter the ordinarily accepted account of Hamilton's birth and parentage, and, after the most careful consideration and investigation which I have been able to give, I am clearly of the opinion that there is no evidence sufficient to justify any biographer in setting it aside. At the same time grave doubts have been cast upon this account, and as they proceeded from so eminent an authority as Mr. Bancroft, I felt that it was impossible for me to pass them over in silence, especially when entirely new material relating to this subject had come to my knowledge. The question of Hamilton's parentage possesses the interest which always attaches to the origin of very distinguished men, and the date of his birth affects our estimate of his youthful powers. On any theory Hamilton displayed great talents at a very early age, but if the accepted date of his birth is correct, his precocity was certainly extraordinary. Mr. Bancroft is evidently of the opinion that Hamilton was older than he was said to have been when he spoke at the meeting in the fields, for he could hardly have " appeared" less than seventeen, which is the age given him by his biographer. Mr. Bancroft's doubts arose partly, perhaps, from the intrinsic improbability of such unusual intellectual maturity, but chiefly from the deed signed by Hamilton as a witness in 1766. If Hamilton was born in 1757, he was only nine years old when he signed this instrument. It is certainly not a little remarkable that a child of that tender age should have been accepted as a competent witness to an important document, but it is not in the least impossible, and any conclusion based on this phenomenon must of course be mere conjecture. If at thirteen he was able to manage the affairs of a considerable merchant, he might very well have been a fit witness at nine. The character of his signature is of more importance than the fact of his affixing it to a deed. I have carefully examined an exact tracing of this signature. The hand-writing is obviously Hamilton's. The signature is written in a fair, open hand, and might well be the work of a man. Only a close examination, which reveals a certain roundness in the letters, and some deliberation on the part of the writer, suggests youthful penmanship. The signature is certainly a very mature one to have been written by a boy nine years old. But then it is not at all an impossible feat, and is by no means so extraordinary as the letter to Ned Stevens a few years later, or, indeed, as many of Hamilton's youthful performances.

This document, signed in 1766, is the only evidence directly bearing on Hamilton's age; but the fact that the date of his birth has been questioned, leads necessarily to an inquiry as to the circumstances of his origin and parentage, which have rendered such doubts possible. In a letter to a kinsman in Scotland, in 1797, he himself says: " You no doubt have understood that my father's affairs at a very early day went to wreck; so as to have rendered his situation during the greatest part of his life ineligible. This state of things occasioned a separation between him and me, when I was very young, and threw me upon the bounty of my mother's relatives, some of whom were then wealthy, though, by vicissitudes to which human affairs are so liable, they have been since much reduced and broken up. I myself, at about sixteen, came to this country." This meagre statement is all Hamilton himself tells us of his origin. He separated completely from his past when he joined the army of the Revolution. We have no letters from relatives or friends in the West Indies except from Dr. Knox, the Nevis clergyman. There is also a letter, dated in 1785, from Hamilton to a brother James, who had written to him for money. In this letter Hamilton says that he has not heard from his brother and correspondent for years, and does not know whether he is married or single. He then asks anxiously about his father, saying that he not only is totally ignorant of that gentleman's circumstances, but that he does not know whether his father is alive or dead.[1] After Hamilton became famous his father appeared, or rather wrote to him, and he sent his father money and urged the old gentleman to come to this country.

This lack of information concerning the family and early life of such an eminent man is of itself enough to cause inquiry, and every one versed in American history is aware of the fact that a certain amount of mystery has hung over Hamilton's birth and parentage. Every student of the period is also familiar with the story, which oral tradition has handed down, that Hamilton was the illegitimate son of a rich West Indian planter or merchant, generally supposed to have been Mr. Stevens, the father of Hamilton's early friend and school-fellow.

This tradition has always been vague and unsupported. In the course of an examination of the Pickering papers for another object, I found among the memoranda collected by Colonel Pickering, with

[1] *History of the Republic*, by J. C. Hamilton, vol. vii. p. 842.

the purpose of writing memoirs of his contemporaries, two somewhat similar accounts of Hamilton's birth and parentage. It must be remembered that, although Colonel Pickering did not always agree with Hamilton, he was one of his most devoted admirers. He considered Hamilton by far the greatest man of his time and country, ranking him without hesitation above Washington. The memoranda in question are as follows : —

ALEXANDER HAMILTON. *Philadelphia, February 15,* 1822.

This morning I met with my friend Mr. James Yard of this city, with whom I have had an acquaintance of between twenty and thirty years. He and Dr. Stevens of the West Indies married, if I mistake not, two sisters, the daughters of the Danish Governor of Santa Cruz, of the name of Walterstorff (or a name sounding like it). Mr. Yard first introduced Dr. Stevens to me, when it was contemplated to appoint him American Consul General for St. Domingo, at the time that the distinguished negro General Toussaint L'Ouverture bore the chief sway in the Island. The conversation led us to speak of General Alexander Hamilton. I remarked to Mr. Yard, that at the first sight of Dr. Stevens his likeness to Hamilton was so strong, I concluded they were brothers, for it was generally understood that Hamilton was an illegitimate son of a gentleman of that name. Mr. Yard now told me that General Hamilton was born in the island of Nevis (near St. Christopher's), the natural son of a Scotch gentleman of the name of Hamilton ; that he was an apprentice to Nicholas Cruger, who afterwards removed (or returned) to New York ; that there Hamilton and Stevens went to school together ; and since the death of Hamilton, an aunt, the sister of his mother, came to New York, and was for some weeks in Mrs. Hamilton's house, from whom (Mr. Yard naturally concluded) Mrs. Hamilton must have received full information of her husband's parentage ; that this aunt being poor, and removed to Burlington, in New Jersey, received the aids of benevolence, partly from Mr. Yard ; who also facilitated her return to the West Indies. Mr. Yard added, that General Hamilton's mother died but two or three years ago.

Mr. Yard told me, that after he knew that the papers, collected in relation to writing the life of Hamilton, had been put into the hands of Mr. Joseph Hopkinson, he advised Hopkinson frankly to state, that Hamilton was the natural son of a Scotch gentleman in the West Indies, as an avowal of a fact for which Hamilton, not being responsible, ought not to suffer in his reputation. [Mr. Yard (a gentleman of distinguished sagacity and information) might also think an open avowal of the fact more dignified in relation to a person of Hamilton's exalted talents and integrity, than any other course ; and that to glide over his birth, the birth of a man so eminent, without adverting to his father, would amount to a confession that he was (in I believe English law-language) "filius nullius," or in plain English, "Nobody knew who was his father," the meaning of both expressions being that he was some one's natural son].

As to the strong likeness between General Hamilton and Dr. Stevens, Mr. Yard could give no account ; altho' it seemed apparent that he thought them near of kin. In cases of this sort, the possibility of *kindred blood* gives rise to surmises, or strong suspicions, of which no proof is attainable. — *From the Pickering MSS. vol. li. p.* 250.

ALEXANDER HAMILTON.   *June* 29, 1822.

Altho' little if anything was publicly spoken, yet it
seemed always to have been understood, among those
who were acquainted with this extraordinary man, that
he was the illegitimate offspring of a Mr. Hamilton, in
the West Indies. Meeting this morning with Mr. James
Yard, — a merchant of Philadelphia whom I have long
known, a gentleman distinguished for his good sense and
information, and who had lived for some time in the
West Indies, and was particularly conversant with the
Danish Islands of St. Thomas and St. Croix, — I renewed
the subject of General Hamilton's parentage, of which
we had before conversed, and Mr. Yard repeated : That
Hamilton was born in the Island of Nevis, the reputed
son of a Scotch merchant of the name of Hamilton.
That he was some time in the store of Mr. Cruger (I believe in St. Croix), and was sent to New York to obtain
an education, it being observed that he possessed a mind
of a superior cast. Mr. Yard supposed that Mr. Cruger
(who was from New York) contributed towards the
means required for that object. Edward Stevens (afterwards Dr. Stevens with whom I was acquainted in this
city) was sent with Hamilton to New York, for the same
purpose — his education.

About the year 1798, after the French had been massa-
cred or expelled from Hispaniola, and the negroes under
Toussaint were masters of the French part of the island,
it was thought expedient by the American Government
(Adams then the President) to send thither an agent,
in the character of Consul General, and from my inquiries concerning Dr. Stevens, then in Philadelphia, he
appeared in all respects singularly qualified for the office.
He had long resided in the West Indies, understood the

French language, was very intelligent, and a worthy man. With his brother-in-law, James Yard (for I understood they had married sisters, the daughters of the Governor Walterstorff of one of the Danish Islands), I had a previous acquaintance; and to him I expressed my opinion of Dr. Stevens, from what I had heard of his character, from Mr. Yard, or some other source of information. The arrangements being thus far advanced, I said to Mr. Yard : " But I have not yet seen Dr. Stevens." Mr. Yard answered, " I will bring him to you." They came together to see me. At the first glance, I was struck with the extraordinary similitude of his and General Hamilton's faces ; I thought they must be *brothers.* To-day, Mr. Yard informed me that the remark had been made a thousand times ; that when young children, they lived together in the family of the father of Stevens, and were sent together to New York for their education. Conjecture here will suppose some secrets, which, if known, might account for the striking likeness of these two persons.

Mr. Hamilton, the reputed father of the General, became a planter in Granada. Whether he patronized, or in any way provided even for the education of Alexander, Mr. Yard did not know. An aunt of Alexander's came from the West Indies to New York, some years ago, and lived a good while in the family of Mrs. Hamilton, the General's widow. Thence the aunt (I think Mr. Yard called her name Mitchell) went to Burlington ; where, becoming blind, a collection was made among some of Hamilton's friends, to enable her to go back to the West Indies. There is now in this city a person (I think Mr. Yard called him a merchant and pronounced his name, but which I do not recollect), Mr. Yard said, the son of another sister of General Hamilton's mother. — *From the*

Pickering MSS. vol. li. p. 302, in possession of the Massachusetts Historical Society.

It does not, of course, in any way detract from Hamilton's fame or from his merits if any of these stories should be true. It is needless to say that such a fact would not reflect upon him, or upon those who bear his name and have the honor to be descended from him. His rise was remarkable, and was equally honorable to his talents and character when it is remembered that he came a stranger from an obscure island, one of the pettiest possessions of England, and that he made his way to the very highest rank in everything which he attempted, unsupported by wealth and unaided by family connections. If, in addition to all the difficulties which he overcame, that of illegitimacy be added, it is simply a new title to the respect of the world for his genius and force of character. One of the penalties of his greatness is the fact that thereby the question of his birth and parentage assumes considerable historical interest.

It can be said that Colonel Pickering's memoranda are mere gossip. Such they are on their face, and nothing would be more distasteful to me than to print them, if they could thus be put aside. They could be condemned in this way if we had a clear, authentic, and well-proved account of Hamilton's origin. As this is not the case, the memoranda of Colonel Pickering, taken in conjunction with the doubts expressed by Mr. Bancroft and the tradition familiar to students of our history, acquire an importance and interest which they would not otherwise possess, and

which render it impossible silently to pass them over
in any attempt to write Hamilton's life.   To explain
clearly what has just been said, it is necessary to look
closely at the accepted account, and show briefly why
it is of such a nature as to make doubts possible and
give importance to Colonel Pickering's statements.

We are not told by Mr. John C. Hamilton, either
in the first and unfinished life of his father or in his
second elaborate and complete life, entitled the " History of the Republic," the Christian name of Hamilton's maternal grandfather, Mr. Faucette, or of Hamilton's mother, or of his mother's first husband.   We
are not told when or where Mrs. Hamilton was married to her first husband, Lavine, from whom it is said
she was divorced.   Divorce was extremely rare in
the colonies.   In England and in the crown provinces
it involved long, difficult, and expensive proceedings
of the greatest publicity.   We are not told when,
where, how, or for what cause the divorce was obtained.   In the first life it is said that "there were
several sons, of whom Alexander was the youngest."
In the "History of the Republic" it is stated that
Hamilton was the only surviving child ; and yet in
the appendix to the same work a letter is given, to
which I have already referred, written by Hamilton
to a brother named James.   If this contradiction is
explained by a second marriage of Hamilton's father,
it can only be said that there is no mention of such
a marriage.   In the first life it is said that Hamilton
was confided to the care of his mother's relatives,
Mr. Peter Lytton and his sister, afterwards Mrs.

Mitchell. In the "History of the Republic," Mr.
Lytton and Mrs. Mitchell have disappeared, and
Hamilton's guardians are spoken of simply as his
mother's relatives. From the Pickering memoranda
we learn that Mrs. Mitchell came to this country and
lived with Hamilton's widow, and that she was a
sister of Hamilton' mother. Mr. Peter Lytton was
therefore the brother of Hamilton's mother, and her
maiden name must have been Lytton and not Faucette, unless there was a second marriage in this instance also, and the relationship between her and
Lytton, therefore, only that of the half-blood. Mr.
John C. Hamilton says that Hamilton's mother died
while Alexander was still a child. Mr. Yard, on
the other hand, who had married into a West Indian family, who was a close connection of Edward
Stevens, Hamilton's earliest friend and school-fellow,
and who was therefore in a position to know, says
that Hamilton's mother was living in 1818. The
unquestioned resemblance between Stevens and Hamilton would be of no great importance, and might
readily be dismissed as accidental, were it not for the
additional fact that they were educated, and went
to college together, and that, according to Mr. Yard,
Hamilton was brought up in the Stevens family.

Enough has been said to show the cause of the
doubts which have existed as to Hamilton's origin,
and also the reason for the interest and importance
which attach to the Pickering memoranda as the
only evidence we have on the point from Hamilton's
contemporaries, and which render their publication

historically desirable and even necessary. All the evidence has now been presented so far as I have been able to collect it, and the readers of this note can draw conclusions from it as well as I can. The various facts from the different sources cannot be reconciled with each other, or formed into a clear and coherent narrative as they stand, but this is probably owing to lack of fullness of statement.

The usually accepted version, which upon all the evidence in our possession I believe to be true, rests on the meagre statement of Hamilton himself which I have quoted, and on the careless and unsupported account given by Mr. John C. Hamilton. It may be fairly said that the authority of Hamilton and of his son is enough on such a matter, and, in the entire absence of convincing proof to the contrary, I have so treated it; and fully admitting the force of this argument, I have accepted their statement in this biography as final. As to the question of age, Hamilton himself could hardly have been much mistaken. He says he was sixteen when he came to this country, and I have no doubt that on any theory of his parentage this statement is correct, or very nearly so. He may fairly be accepted as one of the most remarkable examples of mental precocity of which we have any knowledge. There is also no doubt as to the identity of his father, James Hamilton. He was a younger son of the Laird of Grange, one of the Cambuskeith Hamiltons, and is duly recorded in Patterson's " History of Ayrshire and its Families " (p. 203, vol. i.). Hamilton himself knew about his father's family and the two elder brothers successively Lairds of Grange, and his authority as to his parentage can be overthrown only by direct proof to the contrary.

In conclusion let me say, more definitely if possible than I have yet done, that I have discussed this matter fully, and have printed this note, and the somewhat contradictory Pickering memoranda, solely because I did not feel that it would have been honest for a biographer to suppress such new and important statements, however vague and inconclusive, in regard to the birth and parentage of a man who was so highly distinguished, and who left such deep marks of his personal influence upon the history and institutions of the United States.

NOTE B.

The quarrel between Hamilton and Washington, which led to the former's leaving the staff of the commander-in-chief, has always been given an importance which perhaps does not properly belong to it. It has at all events always been fully discussed by every one who has had occasion to consider it, and I therefore shall be pardoned for adding some facts in regard to it which came to my knowledge after this volume was in the press. It is well known that Hamilton was not fully satisfied with his position on Washington's staff, and that he desired to be appointed adjutant-general, that he was pressed for this post by Lafayette ("Memoirs and Correspondence of Lafayette," vol. i. p. 366) and by General

Greene (Hamilton's "History of the Republic," vol. i,
p. 141), and that Lafayette subsequently wrote to him
in a way which showed that his resignation from the
staff had been contemplated for some time. ("Memoirs and Correspondence of Lafayette," vol. i. p.
302.)

I have been informed by a gentleman [1] who was a
most eminent historical authority, and a friend of the
late Jared Sparks, that Mr. Sparks told him of a
conversation which he had with Lafayette on this
subject when the latter visited this country in 1825.
Lafayette told Mr. Sparks that Hamilton had pressed
Washington for another position; that Washington
had refused his request, as in the case of the adjutant-
generalship; and that they had had two or three dis-
agreements growing out of this wish of Hamilton's
before the final breach at New Windsor. This statement shows that there were causes for the quarrel
which did not appear on the surface, and that the
separation was neither a new nor a sudden idea upon
Hamilton's part at least. (See, also, Hamilton's letter to Schuyler, February 18, 1781, in the new edition
of Hamilton's Works, where it is now for the first
time given in full.)

NOTE C.

Hamilton's argument in the Croswell case was reported and printed in a pamphlet which is occasion-
ally to be met with, and has been reprinted in Moore's
"American Eloquence."

[1] The late Rev. George E. Ellis.

INDEX

INDEX

ADAMS, JOHN, " Discourses on Davila" against Jefferson, 140; election endangered by Hamilton's advice, 193; elected, 194; difficulty of his relations with Hamilton, the real leader, 194–198; suspects Hamilton of intrigue and tries to crush him, 196, 197; considered unsafe by Hamilton, 196; agrees with Hamilton in wishing a French commission, 199; selects commissioners in opposition to Hamilton's advice, 200; his error in so doing, 200, 201; sends X Y Z correspondence to Congress, 201; answers patriotic addresses, 202; sends nomination of Washington and three major generals to Congress, 203; refuses to give Hamilton highest rank, 203, 204; obliged by Washington to submit, 204; his conduct in the affair, 205; thinks Hamilton wishes military conquest, 212; on news of Talleyrand's readiness for reconciliation, nominates Murray minister to France, 214; probably hopes to cripple war party, 214; error of his action, 214, 216, 217; enlarges commission, 217; refuses to delay its departure, 217; favors Alien and Sedition Laws, 220; attacked by Pickering, 226; drives Pickering and McHenry from cabinet, 226; abuses Hamilton, 226; refuses to answer his letters, 226, 227; asks from Hamilton a position for his son-in-law, 227; folly of his treatment of Hamilton, 227, 228; again a candidate for the presidency, 228; attacked in a pamphlet by Hamilton, 229, 230; defeated in election, 232.

Adams, John Quincy, writes " Publicola " against Jefferson, 140.

Adams, Samuel, converted into advocate of Constitution, 73.

Alien and Sedition Acts, passed, 219; responsibility for, 220.

Ames, Fisher, superior as an orator to Hamilton, 78, 269.

André, Major, Hamilton's acquaintance with and sympathy for, 20.

Annapolis convention, called by Virginia, 53; issues address calling for general convention, 54.

Army, of Revolution, neglected by Congress, 39; adopts Newburgh addresses, 40; ready for revolution, 40, 41.

Arnold, Mrs. Benedict, Hamilton's interview with, after her husband's treachery, 20.

Asia, British man-of-war, fires on New York, 10.

Assumption of state debts, struggle over, 118–127. See Congress of the United States.

BACHE, B. F., upholds Genet, 168.

Bancroft, George, doubts as to date of Hamilton's birth, 283, 284.

Bank, suggested by Hamilton under confederacy, 28, 29; report on, to first Congress, 98–102; political reasons for, 102, 103; constitutionality of, defended by Hamilton, 103; debated in Congress, assailed by Jefferson and others, 129.

Bayard, James A., letter of Hamilton to, suggesting methods of building up the Federalist party, 263–265.

Benson, Egbert, Hamilton's colleague at Annapolis convention, 54.

Bimetallism, advocated by Hamilton, 105, 106.

Bland, Theodoric, in Congress of 1782, 35.

Bowdoin, James, crushes Shays's rebellion, 52; leads Massachusetts to urge a new convention, 52.

Burr, Aaron, his alliance with the Livingstons, 81; opinion of Hamilton as a writer,188, 273; first of a line of New York politiicans, 220; his ability as a manager, 223; defeats Hamilton, 223; obtains and prints copy of Hamilton's attack on Adams, 229; intrigues with Federalists to get presidency, 232; prevented from success by Hamilton, 233; a leader of New York bar, 234; defeated in intrigues by Hamilton, 242, 243; and by Jefferson, 243; defeated for governor by Lewis through Hamilton's influence, 243; determines on revenge, and forces a quarrel, 243, 244; his character and real abilities, 244, 245; not a murderer according to code of honor, 245; relieved by Hamilton in pecuniary difficulties, 246; prepares for duel, 246; kills Hamilton, his subsequent fate, 247.

CALLENDER, JAMES T., libel of Croswell against, 236.

"Camillus," essays of, 188, 189.

Carrington, Edward, asked by Hamilton in regard to public feeling in Virginia, 251.

"Christian Constitutional Society," Hamilton's plan for, 264.

Clinton, George, letter of Hamilton to, explaining his course in Congress, 39; urged by Hamilton to provide for paying British debts, 45; dreads a strong central government as a diminution of his power in New York, 51; leads New York to reject a permanent revenue for Congress, 55; fails to prevent call of state convention, 69; secures a majority of delegates, 70; although defeated in convention retains control of State, 79; prevents reëlection of Hamilton to Congress, 79; defeats Yates for governorship, 80; loses control of legislature and State, 80.

Clymer, George, in Continental Congress of 1782, 35.

Code of honor, in Burr-Hamilton case, 244, 245–249.

Coinage, report on, 105; debate as to its device, 127.

Confederacy, condition in 1780, 28, 29; in 1782, 44; degradation in 1786–87, 49–52.

Connecticut, troops from, in New York Tory riots, 10, 11.

Congress, Continental, preparation for in New York, 7, 9; its inefficiency, 28; decay in 1782, 35; its leaders, 35; influenced by Luzerne to place peace negotiations in French hands, 37; defeated in attempt to get an impost from States, 38; recommends grant from the States, 39; its ingratitude toward soldiers, 39, 41; thanks Washington, 41; refuses to open debates to public, 41; standing of Hamilton in, 42; refuses a permanent revenue by New York in 1787, 55; fixes date for operation of Constitution, 79.

Congress of the United States, its slowness in assembling, 81; refers financial questions to Hamilton, 84; debates payment of domestic debt, 115–118; debates assumption of state debt, 118–125; defeats assumption, 121; reverses action through Jefferson's influence, 125, 127; adopts other financial measures, 127; debates question of device on coins, 127; debates and establishes bank, 129; rejects Hamilton's new tax and loan bills, 146; investigates Hamilton's financial integrity, 147, 148; rejects resolutions of censure, 148; debates resolutions for discriminating duties, 173, 174; confirms Jay's nomination as special commissioner to England, 176; passes excise bill, 179; gives executive added powers to crush Whiskey Rebellion, 180; supports Washington in denouncing Democratic societies, 183; investigates Hamilton's administration a second time, 184; Senate ratifies Jay treaty, 186; struggle over it in House, 190; passes acts for defense against France, 202; carried by Federalists, 202; passes act for organizing troops, and others, 206, 207; passes Alien and Sedition Acts, 219; again carried by Federalists, 211; elects Jefferson President over Burr, 232, 233.

Constitution of the United States, Hamilton's plan for, 60, 61; struggle over its adoption, 64–79.

Convention, Federal, suggested by Hamilton in 1780, 28; by New York in 1782, 34; by Massachusetts in 1787, 52; by Annapolis convention, 54; election of delegates to, in New York, 56; Hamilton's action in, 56–62.

Cooper, Dr. Myles, president of King's College, saved from mob by Hamilton, 10, 11.

Croswell, Henry, prosecuted for libel against Jefferson, 236; his condemnation and defense by Hamilton, 236, 237, 238, 296.

Croucher, ——, his evidence broken down by Hamilton in a murder case, 239, 240.

Cruger, Nicholas, apprenticeship of Hamilton with, 287, 289.

DAYTON, JONATHAN, letter of Hamilton to, on necessities of Constitution, 220, 221.

Democratic party, formed in debates on assumption of state debt, 120; its elements, 128; dreads monarchy and aristocracy, 128; its lack of unity in 1789, 135; concentrates upon opposition to Hamilton's financial policy, 136; secretly organized by Jefferson and Madison, 139; given an organ in "National Gazette," 141; attacks Hamilton for corruption, 142; first declaration of programme, 143; attacks Hamilton again in Congress, without success, 146–148; upholds Genet, 168, 169; bases opposition to Federalists on foreign policy, 172; attacks England in Congress, 174; but refuses to prepare for war against her, 175; opposes Hamilton for English mission, 175, 177; discredited by suppression of Whiskey Rebellion, 182; its societies die out, 183; again fails to damage Hamilton by investigation, 184; its anger at Jay's mission, 185; denounces Jay treaty, 186; paralyzed by X Y Z affair, 202; leaves Congress, 218; considered revolutionary by Federalists, 220, 221; its success considered fatal by Hamilton, 225; prosecutes Croswell for libel, 236; felt by Hamilton to threaten revolution in United States, 251, 252, 254, 258, 259, 260, 266, 267; its opinion of Hamilton's ability, 273.

"Democratic societies," founded on model of Parisian clubs, 182; denounced by Washington, 183.

Diplomatic history of the United States: position toward European nations in 1789, 153; mission of Gouverneur Morris to England,

155; negotiations with Hammond over treaty, 156; discussion of neutrality in cabinet, 159-162; mission of Genet, 164-177; Jay's mission to England, 175-177, 185, 186; Monroe's mission to France, 198; rejection of Pinckney by France, 198; mission of Pinckney, Marshall, and Gerry, 200; X Y Z affair, 201; efforts of Talleyrand toward reconciliation, 213, 214; the second commission, 214, 217, 218.

Duane, James, letter of Hamilton to, on weakness of confederacy, 28.

ENGLAND, treaty of peace with, in 1782, 37; refuses to surrender Western posts, 47, 50; seeks to ruin American commerce, 50, 53; its constitution imitated in federal convention, 59; unfriendly relations with, in 1788, 153; policy towards, advocated by Hamilton, 154, 155; sends Hammond as minister, 156; stupid interference of, with commerce, 172; issues "provision order," 174; renews it during excitement over Jay treaty, 189; alliance with, not wished by Hamilton, 215, 257; issues untimely Orders in Council, 215.

Excise, recommended by Hamilton in 1790, 95; objections to and reasons for, 96-98.

FAUCETTE, name of Hamilton's maternal grandfather, 292.

Fauchet, J. A. S., replaces Genet as French minister, 177.

"Federalist," the, its composition, 65, 66; its character, 66, 67; as a literary effort, 67-69.

Federalist party, first formed in debate on payment of domestic debt, 118; its elements, 124, 128, 134; given a programme by Hamilton, 134, 135; forces a vote on

resolutions of censure on Hamilton, 148; its foreign policy, 161; wishes to prepare for war with England, 174, 175; disapproves Jay treaty, 187; selects candidates for presidency and vice-presidency in 1796, 191, 192; discord in, over candidates, 193, 194; elects Adams, but not Pinckney, 194; Adams its nominal leader as President, 194; Hamilton its real leader, 195; one faction of, wishes war with France, 199; after X Y Z, whole party wishes war, 202; sweeps the country in elections, 202; its leaders alarmed at Adams's course in appointment of major-generals, 204; torn in two over Adams's proposed mission to France, 214; anger of extremists against Adams, 215; saved from wreck by Hamilton's advice, 217, 218; success of its foreign policy, 218; misuses its supremacy in Congress, 218, 219; prevented from passing extreme bills by Hamilton, 219; considers Democrats Jacobins, 221; continues to have majority in Congress, 221; dissensions in, 222; loses hold on country, 222, 223; defeated in local elections, 223; its leaders urge sharp practice in New York, 224, 225; quarrels between leaders of, 226, 227; principally ruined by Adams's folly, 228; again nominates Adams, 228; defeated by dissensions, 231, 232; intrigues to elect Burr President instead of Jefferson, 232, 233; breaks up after defeat, 242; scheme for its revival, suggested by Hamilton, 263-265; Hamilton's friends in, 274, 275.

"Fenno's Gazette," organ of Federalists, 141.

Finances of the Revolution, 26; Hamilton's letter on, 26, 27, 29; condition in 1782, 38, 39.

Financial history: organization of

Treasury Department, 85, 86; report on public credit, 87–95; on funding of debt, 91, 92; on sinking fund, 92, 93; report on excise, 95, 96; report on the bank, 98–102; report on the mint, 105; report on manufactures, 107; debate on and adoption of these measures, 115–127, 129; speculation and panic, 131; comments on Hamilton's policy, 131–133; further measures introduced, 145; defeated by Democrats, 146.

Fleming, Major, commands volunteer corps joined by Hamilton, 9.

Florida, its seizure urged by Hamilton, 209, 279.

Foreign policy of the United States, Hamilton's views on, 153–155, 160; adoption of neutrality, 160–161; refusal to join France, 163, 164–166; success of neutrality, 170–173; policy during quasi-war, 215, 216.

France, its troops in Revolution, 20; their liking for Hamilton, 25; abandoned by Franklin and others in treaty of peace, 37; its self-seeking policy in Revolution, 50; its attitude toward the confederacy, 50; popular gratitude toward, in 1789, 153; unfavorable commercial relations, 153; policy toward, advocated by Hamilton, 155; question of relations of United States with, during war with England, 162; treaty obligations with, repudiated, 163, 164; feeling against, caused by Genet's excesses, 169, 170; refuses to receive Pinckney, 198; its treatment of commissioners in X Y Z affair, 201; war with, in 1798, 213; seeks place, 213; called the "Great Monster" by Hamilton, 225.

Franklin, Benjamin, abused for violating instructions in making peace, 36, 37; praised by Hamilton, 37.

Free trade, Hamilton's criticisms of, 110, 112.

French Revolution, its beginnings influence Jefferson, 123; applauded in United States, 157; its excesses alienate Federalists, 158; continues to be admired by Democrats, 158, 168; causes one Federalist wing to wish war with France, 199, 215; its probable failure foreseen in 1789 by Hamilton, 250; its difference from American Revolution insisted on, 253, 254; its influence in America dreaded, 258, 259; plan of Hamilton to counteract, 263, 264.

Freneau, Philip, established by Jefferson as editor of "National Gazette," 141; attacks Hamilton, 141; attacked bitterly by him through "Fenno's Gazette," 143, 144; upholds Genet, 168.

GALLATIN, ALBERT, the only Democratic leader left in Congress after X Y Z affair, 202.

Gates, Horatio, defeats Burgoyne, 18; his great reputation in New England, 18; reluctant to send troops to Washington, persuaded by Hamilton, 19.

Genet, Edmond Charles, arrives as minister from French republic, 164; his character and policy, 165; fits out privateers, 165; journey to Philadelphia, 165; tries to continue sending out privateers, 166; aided by Jefferson in sending out Little Sarah, 167; makes continual demands for money, 167, 168; excited by signs of popular support, 168; becomes increasingly violent, his recall demanded, 169, 170; appeals to people against Washington, 170; loses influence, 170; his effect in creating a party issue, 172; replaced by Fauchet, 177; his influence in founding Democratic societies, 182.

Gerry, Elbridge, appointed on French commission by Adams, 200; his conduct in France, 200, 201.

Giles, William B., leads Jefferson's attack on Hamilton in Congress, 146; introduces resolutions of censure and is defeated, 148; discomfited by X Y Z letters, 202.

Greene, Nathanael, impressed by Hamilton, introduces him to Washington, 13; Hamilton's gratitude and respect for, 13; urges Hamilton for post of adjutant-general, 296.

Grenville, Lord, negotiates treaty with Jay, 175.

HAMILTON, ALEXANDER, birth and ancestry, 1; precocity, 1; education, 2; despises clerkship, 2; manages employer's affairs, 2; attracts attention by description of hurricane, 3; sent by relatives to New York for education, 3; in school at Elizabethtown, 3, 4; his youthful literary activity, 4; studies at King's College, 4; his independent situation in New York, 5; visits Boston in 1774, 6; decides to join side of colonies, 6; speaks to people at patriot meeting in the fields, 7; writes successful pamphlets defending Congress, 9; declines offers from Tories, 9; joins a volunteer corps, 9; saves Dr. Cooper from a patriot mob, 10; also Thurman, 11; angered at patriot attack on Rivington's Tory press, 11; raises and commands an artillery company, 12; drills it successfully, 13.

In the Revolutionary War. Introduced by Greene to Washington, 13; acts with credit in battle of Long Island, 13; also at White Plains, and in the New Jersey campaign, 14; appointed aide on Washington's staff, 14; wisdom of his choice in abandoning line service, 15; his duties as staff officer, 15; conducts Washington's correspondence, 15; not to be considered as responsible for it, 16; great value of his services, 17; growth of his intellect illustrated by the dispatches, 17, 18; sent to Gates to get reinforcements after Saratoga, 18; difficulty of his situation, 19; succeeds in getting troops without causing a rupture, 19; succeeds equally well with Putnam, 19; sent to Newport on unsuccessful mission to French, 19, 20; meets Mrs. Arnold and André at time of West Point affair, 20; his deep feeling for André, 20; resents a reproof from Washington and leaves staff, 21; his youthful pride, 21, 22; repels Washington's advances for reconciliation, 23; storms British redoubt at Yorktown, 23; leaves the army, 24; significance of his military career in developing character, 24; wins warm friends among Americans and French, 25; his military talents, 25, 26.

In Law and Politics. His strong tendency toward government, 26; writes letter to Robert Morris on paper currency, 26, 27; its ability, 27; proposes contraction, taxation, loans, and a bank, 27, 28; wishes to unite moneyed classes in support of the government, 28; writes to Duane on weakness of confederacy, 28, 29; urges assumption of power by Congress, 28; urges same expedients to Sears, 29; again urges bank upon Morris, 29; ahead of his time in these proposals, 30; marries Miss Schuyler, 31; advantages of this family connection, 31, 32; refuses General Schuyler's offers of assistance and studies law, 32; his hasty but effective preparation, 32, 33; declines, in favor of Laurens, to be commissioner of French loan, 33 ; mentioned for peace commissioner, 34 ; appointed receiver of Continental taxes for New York, 34 ; makes vigorous but unsuccessful efforts to get money, 34 ; elected to Congress, 34, 35 ; makes energetic efforts for reform, 36 ; introduces resolution to disclose secret article of treaty of 1782 to France, 37 ; tries to induce Rhode Island to consent to impost scheme, 38 ; opposes recommending a grant for term of years, 39 ; angered at Congressional neglect of army, 39 ; condemns Pennsylvania for not protecting Congress against mutineers, 41 ; draws resolutions of thanks to Washington, 41 ; urges in vain a small permanent army, 41 ; tries to have debates made public, 41 ; retires to private life, 42 ; his reputation increased, 42 ; his early democratic ideas affected by his experience, 43, 44 ; begins to advocate aristocracy and distrust democracy, 44, 45 ; continues active in New York affairs, 45 ; urges payment of British debts, 45 ; defends Tory client against "Trespass Act," 46 ; writes pamphlets advocating amnesty to Tories, 47 ; plan of opponents to murder him, 47 ; helps found a state bank, 47 ; opposes a land bank scheme, 47 ; active in forming the Cincinnati, 47, 48.

Advocate of the Constitution. Plans and secures sending of delegates from New York to Annapolis Convention, 53, 54 ; drafts address of convention calling a new convention to reorganize the government, 54 ; elected to New York legislature, 54 ; advocates granting a permanent revenue to Congress, 55 ; defeated, after hot debate, by Clinton's followers, 55 ; carries resolution to send delegates to Federal Convention, 56 ; elected a delegate with antagonistic colleagues, 56 ; his agitation by letters and pamphlets, 57 ; his impotence in convention, 58 ; concentrates all force on one speech advocating a strong government, 58, 59 ; his aristocratic plan, 59, 60 ; his aim not to secure adoption of plan, but to stimulate convention, 61 ; effect of his speech, 61, 62 ; withdraws from debates, but signs Constitution, 62 ; not entirely satisfied with it, but advocates it vigorously, 63 ; writes " Publius " letters, 65 ; assisted by Madison and Jay in their writing, 66 ; the " Federalist " the main source of his reputation, 67–69 ; leads Federalist minority in New York ratifying convention, 70 ; not discouraged by outlook, 70 ; bitterly attacked, 71 ; his vigorous efforts, 71 ; succeeds in carrying ratification by a majority of three, 72 ; magnitude of his parliamentary victory, 72, 73 ; his high rank as orator, 74, 75 ; elements of his success, 76–79 ; carries through Congress an ordinance to put new government in operation, 79 ; defeated for Congress, 79 ; supports Yates for governor in hopes of defeating Clinton, 79 ; makes an error in not choosing a stronger Federalist, 80 ; causes a rupture with the Livingstons by insisting on election of King as senator, 81 ; evil effect of this blunder, 81.

Secretary of the Treasury. Generally looked upon as proper man for the Treasury, 83 ; sacrifices law practice to accept it, 83, 84; asked by Congress for numerous reports, 84, 85 ; obliged to organize department, 85, 86 ; makes his report on the public credit, 86 ; an important step in his career, 87, 88 ; his main recommendations, 88-95; states objects to be gained by strong credit, 88, 89; their political and centralizing character explained, 89, 90; on funding the debt, 91, 92; absence of trickery in his "sinking fund," 92, 93; defines different classes of debt, 93-95; suggests sundry imposts, 95; in second report urges establishment of excise, 95; his project economically sound, but politically dangerous, 95-97; his purposes, 97, 98; reports on the national bank, 98-105; its educational purpose, 98, 99; intends it to restore business confidence, 100, 101; and to aid the Treasury, 101; his policy still continued, 101, 102; calls upon implied powers to justify constitutionality of the bank, 103; strength of his argument, 103, 104; courage and effectiveness of his step, 104, 105; reports on the mint, 105; advocates a double standard, 105, 106; also a decimal system, 106; his report on manufactures, 107-113; his purpose here also mainly educational, 107; not a follower of Adam Smith, 108; urges necessity of stimulating manufactures, 109; urges economic independence, 110; answers objections, 110, 111; suggests internal improvements, 111; practical character of his reasoning, 112, 113; success of his financial policy in establishing American policy and prosperity, 113, 114; admits cases of occasional injustice in paying domestic debt, 117; abandoned by Madison on question, 117; his centralizing policy detected and attacked, 119, 120; relies on higher classes to sustain him, 120; willing to use situation of capital as make-weight for assumption of state debt, 122; selects Jefferson to aid him, 123; makes arrangement with him, 125; later ac-

cused by Jefferson of deception, 125; absurdity of the charge, 126; succeeds in assumption plan, 127; brings on debate by his suggestion as to device on coinage, 127; carries national bank, 129; writes reply to Jefferson's, Randolph's, and Madison's arguments against the bank, 130; his theories of protection denounced but followed by opponents, 130; tries to discourage speculation, 131; at fault as to rate of interest, 131; weakness of criticisms on his estimates, 131, 132; real value of his financial policy, 132, 133; assumes leadership of Federalists, 134; becomes object of anti-Federalist opposition, 136; accused of "British" sympathies and of being a monarchist, 136; held responsible for speculation and panic, 137; said to have hoodwinked Washington and other Federalists, 137; discovers that Jefferson and Madison are organizing a party against him, 139; attacked by Freneau, 141; his financial measures attacked by Mason, 141; replies in letter to Washington, 142; loses his temper and attacks Freneau, 143; error of his course, 144; exposes Jefferson, 144, 145; at Washington's request, promises to cease, 145; introduces new financial measures to redeem debt, 146; defeated by Democrats, 146; attacked in Congress by Giles for corruption, 146, 147; also by Jefferson, 147; replies with complete success, 147, 148; exhausted by his efforts, 148; fails to impress the rank and file, 149; but stands higher with his party, 150; considers national credit necessary to proper foreign relations, 153; wishes commercial relations with England, 154; advocates impartiality in treatment of foreign countries, 154; an admirer of

English institutions, but not of England, 155; his attitude toward France, 155; good effect of his financial success in England, 155; takes part in negotiations with Hammond, 156; considers himself the prime minister, 156; supported by Washington to the exclusion of Jefferson, 156, 157; loses sympathy with French Revolution, 158; sends for Washington on news of war between France and England, 159; dreads war, 160; thinks question more safely handled by executive than Congress, 160; submits outline of neutrality policy to cabinet, 160; his share in its adoption by the country, 161; advocates caution toward new French government, 162; holds that country is not bound by previous treaties, 163; wisdom of his argument, 164; advocates prevention of privateering by French in American waters, 165; urges severe measures in Little Sarah case, 166; resists Genet's demands on the Treasury, 167, 168; writes "Pacificus" papers defending neutrality, 169; urges peremptory demand for recall of Genet, and publication of correspondence, 169, 170; defeated by Jefferson, 170; wishes to suspend Genet from his functions, 170; success of his policy, 170, 171; opposes, on party grounds, sending Hammond correspondence to Congress, 173; supplies Smith with a speech against Madison's proposal to discriminate in duties against England, 174; urges active measures against England after "Provision Order," 174; suggests a special mission to England, 175; urged by Washington to go, 175; recommends Jay, 176; drafts his instructions, 176; would probably have made a good commissioner,

176; reasons why Democrats opposed him, 177; continues, owing to French Revolution, to fear Democracy, 177, 178; considers his views confirmed by Whiskey Rebellion, 178; tries to render execution of excise law easy, 179; ready, in 1792, for force, 179; drafts a proclamation for Washington, 180; prepares measures of repression, 180; accompanies the expedition, 181; his forbearance toward insurgents, 181, 182; fears Democrat clubs, 183; sustains Washington in his denunciation of them, 183; demands further inquiry into his conduct, 184; passes successful scrutiny, 184; resigns, owing to private affairs, 184.

Leader of the Federalist Party. Does not fear the agitation against Jay, 185; disappointed by treaty, 186; attempts in vain to defend it in New York, 187; writes "Camillus" papers in its defense, 188; their effectiveness, 188; indignant with English provision order, 189; counsels Washington to ratify treaty, 190; aids him by letters and in press, 190, 191; not the leader of the people, 191; an unsuitable candidate for presidency, 191; does not consider himself a candidate, 192; urges equal voting for Adams and Pinckney, 193; indifferent to possibility of election of Pinckney, 193; probably prefers Pinckney, 193; error of his policy, 194; lack of harmony between him and Adams, 195; his view of Adams, 196; anxious to retain leadership, 196; not a difficult person to deal with, 197; on Adams's refusal to consult, tries to force him, 197, 198; dislikes French republic, but wishes to avoid war if possible, 199; agrees substantially as to policy with Adams, 199; wishes him to place Madison or Jefferson on the French mission, 200; wishes rigid instructions, 201; nominated ranking major-general by Washington in provisional army, 203; refused the leading position by Adams, 203; eventually receives it, 204; behaves well, as a rule, although too self-assertive, 205; begins work of organization, 205; his plans approved by Washington, 205, 206; sends a bill to Congress, 206; makes other recommendations, 207; advises the cabinet secretaries, 207; admirable character of his work, 208; plans campaign in the Southwest, 209; always an advocate of free Mississippi navigation and westward expansion, 209; statesmanship of his views, 210; his large views of the ascendency of the United States in America, 210, 211; interested in Miranda's schemes against Spanish America, 211, 212; but does not commit himself to their support, 212, 213; does not wish war with France, 215; nor alliance with England, 215; disgusted at Adams's proposed mission, 216; checks anger of Federalists, and advises a commission of three, 217; urges delay upon Adams, 217; urges modification of first drafts of Alien and Sedition Acts, 219; supports them as passed, 219, 220; does not think Democrats revolutionists, but fears them as dangerous, 220; urges a repressive policy, 221; wishes Congress to condemn Virginia and Kentucky Resolutions, 222; makes strenuous efforts to carry New York, 223; beaten by Burr, 223; proposes to Jay to summon special session of legislature and give election of electors to districts, 224; unscrupulous character of the scheme, 224; driven to it by fear of the revolu-

tionary tendencies of Democrats, 225; called a British sympathizer by Adams, 226; writes courteously, asking to be exonerated, 226, 227; gives Adams's son-in-law a place in the army, 227; again advises an equal vote for Adams and Pinckney, 228; probably means to elect Pinckney, 229; writes a pamphlet attacking Adams, 229; its theft and publication by Burr, 229; its folly, 229, 230; receives information from cabinet officers, 230; not guilty of bad faith, 230, 231; causes defeat of Adams, 231; prevents Federalists in Congress from choosing Burr President over Jefferson, 232, 233.
Professional Life. Profits by laws against Tories to become leader of the bar, 234; after Jefferson's election leaves public life, 235; achieves high success as a jury lawyer, 235; defends Croswell against Democratic prosecution for libel, 236; description of his argument, 237, 238; breaks down testimony of Croucher in a murder case, 238-240; his great success as a jury lawyer due to his reasoning power, 240, 241; emotional, but not rhetorical, 241, 242; baffles Burr's intrigues with the Federalists, 243; denounces schemes of secession, and breaks up coalition of Burr with New York Federalists, 243; not anxious to fight Burr, but accepts his challenge, 244; recognizes the duelist's code, 245; willing to answer to Burr for what he had said, 245, 246; aids Burr in pecuniary difficulties, 246; prepares for the duel, 246; killed by Burr, 247; popular indignation at his death, 247; leaves statement of his reasons for fighting, 248; discussion of them, 249-268; as early as 1789 dreads evil results from

French Revolution, 250, 251; anxious as to Revolutionary feeling in Virginia, 251; and elsewhere, 252; denies any real analogy between American and French revolutions, 252–254; begins to dread outbreaks in New York, 254; advocates strict impartiality in foreign relations, 255, 256; opposes an alliance with England, 257; declines appointment to U. S. Senate on personal grounds, 257; but admits a crisis may arise to call him forth, 258; fears intention of Democrats to make United States a mere province of France, 258; alarmed at Southern sectionalism, 259; wishes to have an army ready to suppress insurrection, 259, 260; in 1799 thinks time has come to attack Democratic party in every way, 260, 261; urges Hoffman to prosecute libelous Democratic newspapers, 260, 261; despondent at collapse of Federalists, 261, 262; thinks his efforts wasted, 262; suggests policy for Federalists to pursue to regain lost ground, 263–265; urges them to appeal to passions and vanity of men, 264; proposes a Christian Constitutional Society, 264; wishes to employ philanthropy and a campaign of education in cities, 265; opposes disunion as not a real remedy for democracy, 266; apprehends an outbreak of anarchy, 266, 267; expects to be the man to lead forces of order, 267; his great error, 267; fights Burr in order to avoid imputations on his courage when the crisis should come, 267, 268. *Character and Services.* Publicity of his entire life, 268, 269; personal appearance, 269, 270; eloquence, 269; power over men, 270, 271; beloved in private life, 271; self-confidence, 271, 272; strong passions, 272; opinion of

his abilities held by opponents, 273; compared to Webster, 273, 274; statements of Kent, 274; character and fidelity of his friends, 275; either loved or hated, 275; not a manager of men, 275; not able to follow, 275; independence, obstinacy, and boldness, 276; his manly action in the Reynolds affair, 276; nature of his ambition, 277; cares for achievement, not office, 277; success of his life, 277; a representative of ideas, 278; an opponent of democracy, 278; an advocate of nationality, 279; influence of his ideas on United States history and institutions, 280; versatility and strength of his character, 281; his standing in history, 281; discussion of his age and parentage, 282–295; alleged by Bancroft to have been older than he himself admits, 283, 284; question as to his signature of a deed in 1766, 284, 285; his own statement, 285; dealings in later life with relatives, 286; said by tradition to have been illegitimate, 286; statements of Yard, according to Pickering, concerning Hamilton's illegitimate parentage, 287–291; these statements evidently mere gossip, 291; conflicting statements of J. C. Hamilton, 292, 293; probable truth of Hamilton's own assertions, 294, 295; his leaving Washington's staff the result of dissatisfied ambition, 295, 296. *Characteristics.* General sketch, 269–281; unfavorable views, 142, 147, 273; ambition, 2, 83, 191, 277; audacity and courage, 7, 10, 11, 13, 14, 17, 70, 177, 244–246, 276; charm of manner, 25, 56; coolness, 13; directness, 126, 127, 241, 276; eloquence, 7, 8, 59, 72, 74–79, 137, 148, 241; energy, 4, 13, 34, 36, 55, 77, 78, 170, 180, 181,

201, 223; generosity, 246, 271; imperiousness, 80, 126, 205; integrity, 147, 230, 231; justice, 6, 45–47; lack of managing ability, 19, 81, 126, 148, 149, 193, 194, 223, 275; lack of popularity, 24, 43, 149; keenness of mind, 17, 19, 61, 63, 217; leadership, 56, 71–75, 134, 136, 191, 195, 217, 233, 242, 275; legal ability, 235–242; literary ability, 9, 15, 16, 17, 65, 69, 114, 188; military ability, 26; organizing skill, 85, 265–268; partisanship in politics, 173, 224, 225; passionateness, 80, 113, 229, 230, 272, 276; personal appearance, 269–271; precocity, 1, 2, 12, 15, 284; self-confidence, 14, 17, 21, 70, 156, 176, 271, 272; self-control, 14, 181, 187, 216, 233; sympathy, 20, 77, 271; systematic habits, 33.

Political Opinions. His place in United States history, 132, 133, 184, 277–281; absence of local feeling, 122; respect for law, order, and authority, 6, 10, 11, 12, 43, 89, 215; on American feeling, 249, 278, 279; aristocracy, 60, 90, 128, 278; assumption of state debts, 95; bimetallism, 106; British Constitution, 59, 136, 155; confederation, 28, 29, 39, 44, 54, 60; Constitution, 60, 62, 63, 65–67, 179, 264, 266; centralization, 28, 29, 44, 60, 221; democracy, 45, 61, 177–179, 215, 267; Democratic party, 183, 220, 225, 251, 254, 258–261, 266–267; disunion, 222, 243, 266; England, 154, 174, 189, 215, 255, 257; excise, 95–97, 179; finances of the confederation, 26, 27, 38, 39; France, 154, 155; French mission, 199, 225, 250, 252, 253; French Revolution, 158, 163, 178, 199, 215; funding debt, 91, 92, 131, 146, 184; foreign policy, 153–155, 159–160, 163, 164, 165, 166, 169, 171, 256; implied powers of Constitution, 103–105,

130; Jay treaty, 186, 187, 190; national bank, 28, 29, 98–101; national government, 88, 89, 97, 101, 104, 114, 122, 182; paper money, 27, 47; party management, 264, 265; protection, 107–113, 130; public credit, 86–95; sinking fund, 92, 93, 146; standing army, 41, 259; Tories, 45–47; treaty of peace, 37; western expansion, 208–213.

Hamilton, James, father of Alexander Hamilton, doubts as to his paternity, 288–294; his identity, 294.

Hamilton, James, writes to Alexander Hamilton for money, 286; Hamilton's reply, 286; his existence apparently ignored by J. C. Hamilton, 292.

Hamilton, John C., fails to throw light on youth of his father, 2; contradictory statements concerning his ancestry, 292, 293.

Hammond, George, first British minister to United States, 156; his negotiations, 156; protests against Genet's actions, 165.

Hancock, John, opposes strong central government as dangerous to his local leadership, 51; resigns governorship, 52; converted from opposition to Constitution, 73.

Higginson, Stephen, in Continental Congress of 1782, 35; votes with Hamilton against recommending grants, 39.

Hoffman, Josiah O., attorney-general, urged by Hamilton to prosecute a Democratic paper, 260.

IMPLIED POWERS, involved in Hamilton's plan of a bank, 103; his defense of them, 103, 104, 130; involved in report on manufactures, 107; denied by Jefferson, Madison, and Randolph, 129.

JAY, John, assists in writing "Federalist," 66; supports Hamilton in New York convention, 70 ; sent on special mission to England, 176 ; inferior to Hamilton in firmness and audacity, 177 ; popular feeling against, after treaty, 187 ; unsuitable as candidate for presidency, 192 ; refuses to adopt Hamilton's proposal to defeat the will of New York, 224 ; wishes to appoint Hamilton to fill vacancy in Senate, 257 ; letter of Hamilton to, on " crisis," 258.

Jay treaty : Jay's mission, 175, 177, 185 ; condemnation of treaty, 186–188 ; ratification of treaty, 190.

Jefferson, Thomas, returns to America from Paris, 123 ; doubtful whether to oppose or support the Constitution, 124 ; helps Hamilton to secure assumption of state debt, 125 ; later claims he was outwitted, 125, 126 ; absurdity of the statement, 126 ; gives Washington an opinion against constitutionality of the bank, 130 ; plans " allowances " for fisheries, and denounces protection, 130 ; decides to oppose policy of administration, 137, 138 ; adopts cautious methods, 138 ; furnishes party name, organization, and catchwords, 139 ; his success as a party builder, 140 ; prints Paine's " Rights of Man " with preface attacking Adams, 140 ; tries to explain it away, 141 ; helps Freneau to found " National Gazette," 141 ; deprecates to Washington Hamilton's measures, 141 ; stirs up others to attack them, 141 ; attacked by Hamilton, 143 ; feels the attack keenly, 144, 145 ; complains of it to Washington, 145 ; plans to prove Hamilton guilty of corruption, 146, 147 ; realizes complete failure of attack, 150 ; fails to obtain commercial advantages from France, 153 ; hampered by Washington's

preference' for Hamilton, 157 ; loves France and hates England, but dreads war, 159 ; advises Washington to throw responsibility on Congress, 159 ; advocates close connection with France, 164 ; opposes compensation for French prizes, 166 ; allows Genet to send Little Sarah to sea, 167 ; privately upholds him, 169 ; opposes publication of Genet correspondence, 169, 170 ; prevents suspension of Genet, 170 ; effect of his course in the whole affair, 171 ; his defeats and false position lead to resignation, 172 ; sends Genet and Hammond correspondence to Congress with report on commerce, 173 ; ability of his correspondence, 173 ; signs but disapproves proclamation against excise riots, 180 ; on Hamilton's opinion of Jay treaty, 186 ; disturbed by Hamilton's " Camillus " papers, 188 ; urges Madison to reply, 188 ; elected Vice-President, 194 ; his nomination on peace commission urged by Hamilton, 200 ; overwhelmed by publication of X Y Z letters, 202 ; carries out Hamilton's plans in acquiring Louisiana, 210 ; looked upon as a Jacobin in New England, 220 ; writes Kentucky resolutions, 222 ; elected President over Burr by House of Representatives through Hamilton's influence, 233 ; Croswell sued for libel against, 236 ; determines to ruin Burr, 243 ; opinion of Hamilton's abilities, 273 ; sustained by Hamilton in acquisition of Louisiana, 279 ; representative of theories opposed to Hamilton's, 279 ; partial success of, 280.

KENT, JAMES, description of Hamilton's argument in the Croswell case, 237, 238 ; on his abilities, 274.

Kentucky, breaks off from Virginia, 50 ; its resolutions in 1798, 222.

King, Rufus, chosen Senator from New York at Hamilton's dictation, 81 ; as minister to England consulted by Hamilton concerning Miranda, 212 ; letter of Hamilton to, on national feeling, 255.

King's College, studies of Hamilton at, 4 ; its president mobbed as a Tory, 10, 11.

Knox, Hugh, gives Hamilton letters to New York, 3 ; letters to Hamilton from, 286.

Knox, Henry, urges strong measures in case of Little Sarah, 166; appointed major-general in provisional army, 203 ; refuses to serve under Hamilton, 204.

LAFAYETTE, MARQUIS DE, his friendship for Hamilton, 25 ; his motives in aiding America, 50 ; letter of Hamilton to, on dangers of failure of French Revolution, 250 ; explains causes of Hamilton's leaving Washington's staff, 295, 296.

Lansing, John, Jr., chosen delegate to federal convention, 56 ; opposes Constitution in New York convention, 70.

Laurens, John, says Hamilton held " pen of Junius," as Washington's aide, 17 ; appointed commissioner of French loan through Hamilton's withdrawal in his favor, 33.

Legislature of New York, controlled by Tories, 7 ; attempt to influence by patriots, 7 ; orders raising of artillery company, 12 ; advocates a better union of States, 34; refuses to adopt tax reform, 34 ; elects Hamilton to Congress, 34 ; passes acts oppressive to Tories, 46, 47 ; denounces judges for decision in Trespass Act case, 46; elects delegates to Annapolis convention, 54 ; refuses a perma-

nent revenue to Congress, 55; elects delegates to Constitutional Convention, 56 ; calls a state convention, 69 ; refuses to reëlect Hamilton to Congress, 79 ; refuses to choose presidential electors, 79 ; carried by Federalists, 80 ; elects senators, 80, 81 ; appropriates money for defense of New York harbor, 205.

Lewis, Morgan, opposes King as Senator from New York, 80, 81 ; his opinion in Croswell libel case, 236, 237 ; elected governor of New York over Burr, 243.

" Liberty Boys," in New York, mob the Tories, 10.

Little Sarah case, 166, 167.

Livingston, Robert R., his plan for a land bank defeated by Hamilton, 47 ; supports Hamilton in state convention, 70.

Livingston family, its hold on New York, 80 ; advocates Constitution, 80 ; opposes King for senator, 81 ; quarrels with Hamilton and his friends, 81.

Long Island, battle of, 13.

Louisiana, its acquisition urged by Hamilton, 209, 257, 279.

Luzerne, Chevalier de, leads Congress to place peace negotiations under French control, 37.

Lytton, Peter, Hamilton's uncle, 292.

MADISON, JAMES, in Continental Congress of 1782, 35 ; assists in writing " Federalist," 66 ; advocates discrimination in domestic debt, 117 ; begins to yield to Virginia sentiment against Federalists, 117, 118 ; argues against constitutionality of bank, 129 ; plans "allowances" for fisheries, denounces protection, 130 ; aids Jefferson in organizing opposition, 139 ; plans to convict Hamilton of corruption, 146 ; humiliated by voting for resolutions of censure on Hamilton, 148; introduces resolutions for discriminating duties against England, 173; opposes appointment of Hamilton on mission to England, 175; declines to enter controversy against Hamilton, 188; his nomination on peace commission urged by Hamilton, 200; looked upon as a Jacobin in New England, 220.

Manufactures, Hamilton's report on, 107.

Marshall, John, his opinion on constitutionality of bank compared with Hamilton's, 103, 104; appointed by Adams on French commission, 200; his return after X Y Z affair, 202; sustains Adams in affair of French mission, 222; ranks Hamilton next to Washington, 281.

Maryland, commercial convention with Virginia, 53.

Mason, Col., criticises policy of administration, 141; answered by Hamilton, 142.

Massachusetts, quarrels with New York, 51; suppresses Shays's Rebellion, 51, 52; calls for a new convention, 52; struggle in, over ratification of Constitution, 73.

McHenry, James, describes standing of Hamilton in Congress, 42, 43; as secretary of war asks Hamilton's advice, 207; driven by Adams from cabinet, 226.

Mint, Hamilton's report on, 105-107.

Miranda, Francisco de, plans for revolution in South America, 211; his relations with Hamilton, 212, 213.

Mississippi, navigation of, upheld by Hamilton in Continental Congress, 209.

Mitchell, Mrs., aunt of Hamilton, her visit to New York, 288, 290, 292, 293.

Monroe, James, not the real author of "Monroe doctrine," 161; opposes selection of Hamilton for English mission, 175; career in France recalled, 198; connection with Reynolds affair, 276.

"Monroe doctrine," really established by Washington's administration, 161; its widest extension foreseen by Hamilton, 210, 211.

Morris, Gouverneur, praises Hamilton's speech at federal convention, 58; warns Hamilton of difficulties of Treasury Department, 83; on importance of finance in United States history, 113; sounds England on renewal of diplomatic relations, 155; despondent letter of Hamilton to, 261.

Morris, Robert, letters of Hamilton to, on finances of confederation, 26, 29; appoints Hamilton Continental tax-receiver for New York; 34; resigns from Treasury, 38; urges Hamilton for secretary of treasury, 83.

Murray, William Vans, nominated by Adams minister to France, 214; member of peace commission, 217.

"NATIONAL GAZETTE," founded by Jefferson to attack Federalists, 141; attacked by Hamilton, 143, 145.

Newburgh addresses, 40; their importance, 40, 41.

New England, admiration for Gates after Saratoga, 18; condemns Jay treaty, 187; its leaders wish war with France, 199; considers Jefferson and Madison Jacobins, 220; plans secession, 243.

New Jersey, gives general powers to Annapolis delegates, 54.

New York, strength of Tories in, 6, 7; mobs in, against Tories, 10, 11; attempt of Hamilton to reform taxation in, 34; hatred of Tories in, 45; quarrels with other States, 51, 52, 53; importance of adhesion to Constitution, 64, 65; opposition in, to new Constitution,

65 ; convention in, 69, 70 ; parties in, 70 ; struggle in convention, 70–72 ; victory of Federalists, 72 ; its importance, 72–75 ; celebration of ratification in, 78 ; demands a new convention, 79 ; unrepresented in first Congress, 79 ; election of Clinton over Yates as governor, £0 ; mob in, against Jay treaty, 187 ; carried by Burr for Democrats against Hamilton, 223 ; scheme of Hamilton for repairing loss, 224, 225 ; attempt of Burr to gain governorship of, defeated by Hamilton, 243.

New York, Assembly of. See Legislature.

New York, Convention of. See Legislature.

Nicholas, John, offers amendment to discriminating duties, naming England, 174.

North Carolina, postpones ratification of Constitution, 74 ; enters Union and defeats assumption of state debt, 121 ; opposes excise law, 179 ; submits, 180.

OTIS, H. G., letter of Hamilton to, on need of a standing army to repress revolution, 259.

"PACIFICUS," essays of, 169.

Paine, Thomas, an edition of his "Rights of Man" published by Jefferson, 140.

Pennsylvania, censured by Congress for failing to protect it against mutineers, 41 ; Wyoming question in, 51 ; " political putrefaction " in, according to Hamilton, 178 ; resists excise law, 179, 180 ; rebellion in, suppressed, 180–182 ; carried by Democrats, 223.

Pickering, Timothy, leader of New England Federalists, 199 ; wishes war with France, 199 ; attacks Adams, 226 ; driven from cabinet, 226 ; letter of Hamilton to, on Great Britain, 257 ; his admira-

tion of Hamilton, 287 ; memoranda concerning Hamilton's birth, 287–291.

Pinckney, Charles Cotesworth, refused reception as minister to France, 198 ; appointed on peace commission, 200 ; appointed major-general in provisional army, 203 ; accepts, without questioning, Hamilton's higher rank, 204 ; confers over organization of army, 206 ; nominated for Vice-President, 228 ; preferred by Hamilton to Adams, 229 ; refuses to be separated by South Carolina from Adams, 231, 232.

Pinckney, Thomas, qualifications as candidate for presidency, 192, candidate for vice-presidency, 192, 193 ; possibility of his election as President according to Hamilton's scheme, 193 ; preferred by Hamilton to Adams, 193, 194 ; defeated, 194.

Pitt, William, compared with Hamilton, 7, 27, 78, 92, 93.

Protection, Hamilton's advocacy of, 107–113 ; favored by first Congress, 130.

Public credit, Hamilton's report on, 89–95.

"Publius," essays of, 65.

Putnam, Israel, made to hurry his troops by Hamilton, 19.

RANDOLPH, EDMUND, criticises Hamilton's draft of address of Annapolis Convention, 54 ; gives Washington written argument against the bank, 129.

Republicans, name at first adopted by Jefferson's followers, 139. See Democratic party.

Revolution, War of, part played by Hamilton in, 13–24 ; battle of Long Island, 13 ; White Plains, 14 ; Trenton campaign, 14 ; correspondence of, 15, 16 ; dealings of Washington with Gates, 18, 19 ; with French, 20 ; Yorktown, 23.

Reynolds, Mrs., affair of, 276.
Rhode Island, refuses to grant Congress an impost, 38 ; refuses to call convention to ratify Constitution, 74.
Rivington, James, Tory printer, his press destroyed by Whigs, 11.

SCHUYLER, MISS ELIZA, letters of Hamilton to, describing Arnold's treachery, 20 ; marries Hamilton, her character, 31.
Schuyler, General Philip, his position and character, 31 ; likes Hamilton, his son-in-law, 32 ; offers to assist him, 32 ; elected senator from New York, 80; defeated by Burr, 81.
Sears, Isaac, letter of Hamilton to, on needs of confederacy, 29.
Sedgwick, Theodore, letter of Hamilton to, opposing disunion, 266.
Shays's Rebellion, 51, 52 ; its influence, 52.
Smith, Adam, Hamilton's familiarity with his writings and his opinion of them, 108.
Smith, Melancton, heads opposition to Constitution in New York Convention, 70 ; admits absurdity of conditional ratification, 72 ; admits that he is convinced by Hamilton, 72; significance of his statement, 75.
Smith, Colonel William, given a position by Hamilton at Adams's request, 227.
Smith, William, of South Carolina, furnished by Hamilton with speech on discriminating duties, 174 ; letter of Hamilton to, on national policy, 256.
Spain, contemptuous attitude toward confederacy, 50 ; difficulties with, over Mississippi, 153 ; success of Pinckney's treaty with, 192; attack upon its American possessions planned by Hamilton, 209 ; schemes of Miranda against, 211-213.

Sparks, Jared, authority for Lafayette's story of Hamilton's leaving Washington's staff, 296.
Spencer, Ambrose, description of Hamilton, comparison with Webster, 273, 274.
Stevens, Edward, letter of Hamilton to, 2 ; supposed to be Hamilton's illegitimate brother, 286, 287 ; his resemblance to Hamilton, 287, 288, 290.
Stoddert, Benjamin, asks Hamilton's advice, 207.

TALLEYRAND, CHARLES MAURICE DE, seeks to reëstablish friendly relations with United States after X Y Z affair, 213.
Thurman, ——, saved by Hamilton from "Travis's mob," 11.
Tories, strong in New York, 6 ; have pamphlet controversy with Hamilton, 8, 9 ; try in vain to win Hamilton, 9 ; mobbed, 10, 11 ; hated in New York after war, 45 ; legislation against, 46, 47 ; defended by Hamilton, 47 ; their proscription enables Burr and Hamilton to control law practice in New York, 234.
"Travis's mob," opposed by Hamilton in attacking Thurman, 11.
Treasury Department, organization of, 84-86.
Treaty of peace, censure of American commissioners for manner of making, 37.
Trenton, campaign of, 14.
Troup, Robert, helps Hamilton to save Dr. Cooper from mob, 10 ; warns him of trials of Treasury Department, 83.
Turgot, compared with Hamilton, 27.

VIRGINIA, withdraws agreement to give Congress an impost, 38 ; wishes commercial retaliation against England, 52; calls Annapolis Convention, 53 ; struggle in, over ratification of Constitution, 74; demands a new convention, 79; its state-rights sentiment affects Madison, 117; opposition in, to excise law, 179; submits, 180.

WASHINGTON, GEORGE, meets Hamilton, through Greene, 13; saves army from Long Island, 14; refuses to permit Hamilton to storm Fort Washington, 14; appoints Hamilton an aide, 14; employs Hamilton to conduct his correspondence, 15; but remains the real author of it, 16; his high estimate of Hamilton's ability, 17; wishes to avoid difficulties with Gates, 18, 19; sends Hamilton on mission to get troops, 19; approves his action, 19; reproves Hamilton for dilatoriness, 21; real kindliness of his action, 22; his interest in Hamilton not diminished by the quarrel, 23; fears evil consequences from neglect of soldiers by Congress, 39; warns Hamilton against using army to threaten Congress, 40; checks movement at Newburgh, 40; importance of his action, 40, 41; thanked by Congress, 41; one of few to think "continentally," 48; effect of his influence in Virginia in behalf of the Constitution, 74; elected President, 81; decides upon Hamilton for Treasury Department, 83; convinced by Hamilton of constitutionality of bank, 103, 130; said by Democrats to be hoodwinked by Hamilton, 137; assailed by Jefferson and Mason with criticisms of Hamilton's conduct, 141, 142; submits Mason's complaints to Hamilton, 142; grieved at newspaper controversy of Hamilton and Jefferson, 145; tries to induce both to cease, 145; his foreign policy, 151; sounds England

as to renewal of diplomatic relations, 155; approves Hamilton rather than Jefferson, 156, 157; loses sympathy with French Revolution, 158; sent for by Hamilton at outbreak of English and French war, 159; approves Hamilton's policy of neutrality, 160, 161; real author of Monroe doctrine, 161; adopts Hamilton's views as to treatment of French privateers, 166; indignant at Jefferson's weakness in Little Sarah case, 167; sympathizes with Hamilton, but refrains from severe measures against Genet, 170, 171; decides to submit Hammond correspondence to Congress as well as Genet's, 173; approves plan of special mission to England, 175; wishes to nominate Hamilton, 175; but, to prevent discord, selects Jay, 176; reasons for so doing, 176, 177; issues proclamation against excise riots, 180; calms troubles in South, 180; calls for troops to crush Whiskey Rebellion, 181; leads the expedition, 181; denounces Democratic societies, 183; unmoved by clamor against Jay treaty, 187; irritated by English provision order, 189; consults Hamilton as to signing treaty, 190; ratifies treaty with protest against provision order, 190; withdraws from politics, 191; his success in managing Hamilton, 197; accepts command of provisional army, 203; nominates major-generals, 203; obliges Adams to accept Hamilton as the first, 204; accepts Hamilton's plans for organization, 206; letter of Hamilton to, on Democratic party, 258; only man beside Hamilton to perceive destiny of United States, 279.

Washington, city, question of its site used as material for bargain by Hamilton, 121, 122; traded to

South for assumption of state debt, 122, 125.

Washington, Fort, offer of Hamilton to recapture by storm, 14.

Webster, Daniel, compared to Hamilton, 273.

West, expansion of United States toward, foreseen by Hamilton, 209, 210, 279.

West Point, Arnold's treachery at, 20; question of its purchase referred to Adams, 85; Academy at, established, 208.

Whiskey Rebellion, causes, 178, 179; proclamations against, 180; increasing violence of, 180; suppression, 181; significance of, 182.

White Plains, battle of, 14.

Wilson, James, in Congress of 1782, 35.

Wolcott, Oliver, asks Hamilton's advice as secretary of the treasury, 207; letter of Hamilton to, on Democratic party, 254; and on France, 256.

X Y Z correspondence sent to Congress, 201.

YARD, JAMES, account of Hamilton's birth and parentage, 287-291.

Yates, Robert, chosen delegate to Federal Convention, 56; opposes Constitution in New York Convention, 70.

Yorktown, Hamilton at siege of, 23.